THE IMPENDING DRAMA

companion volume to *The Key to Victory*

by the author of *Preparation for the Final Crisis*

Fernando Chaij

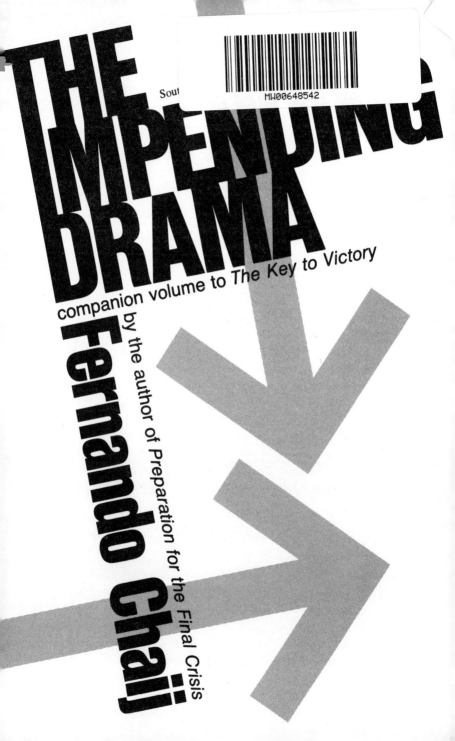

Copyright © 1979 by
Southern Publishing Association

This book was
Edited by Gerald Wheeler
Designed by Mark O'Connor

Type set: 10/11 Palatino

Printed in U.S.A.

Library of Congress Cataloging in Publication Data

Chaij, Fernando.
  The impending drama.

  1. End of the world.   2. Christian life—Seventh-day
Adventist authors.   I. Title.
BT876.C46   248'.48'673   78-22061
ISBN 0-8127-0208-5

Contents

Introduction

The subjects we will deal with in these studies involve not only important prophetic facts and historic events but deep spiritual truths vitally connected with having a daily radiant and happy Christian experience. And finally, they concern our readiness to step into the eternal kingdom of God for an unending life of joy.

This book may answer many questions that we have had for years regarding time, sequence, and nature of some of the climactic events of the last days. Many doubts regarding the actual possibility of achieving a real victorious experience will disappear. And under the guidance of the Holy Spirit a greater desire to reach the utmost role of our life will spring up in our hearts.

We live in an hour of great danger. Satan has committed himself to destroy us. One of his most effective means of attacking us is to submerge us in the lukewarm waters of indifference. Then he can throw us into a state of Laodicean stupor at the precise moment when the True Witness brings us a fervent message of repentance, revival, and reformation.

Shall we allow him to keep us in a state of Laodicean lethargy? Ellen G. White wrote, "The rebuke of God is upon us because of our neglect of solemn responsibilities. His blessings have been withdrawn because the testimonies He has given have not been heeded by those who professed to believe them. Oh, for a religious awakening! The angels of God are going from church to church, doing their duty; and Christ is knocking at the door of your hearts for entrance. But the means that God has devised to awaken the church to a sense of their spiritual destitution have not been regarded. The voice of the True Witness has been heard in reproof, but it has not been obeyed. Men have chosen to follow their own way instead of God's way because self was not crucified in them. Thus the light has had but little effect upon minds and hearts.

"Will the people of God now arouse from their carnal lethargy? Will they make the most of present blessings and warnings, and let nothing come between their souls and the light God would have shine upon them?" (5T 719, 720).

We do not lack information and admonitions in the inspired records of the Bible and in the writings of Ellen White, but somehow the enemy has succeeded in leading us to disregard them.

Time is running out. Practically all the prophetic panorama of the Bible is already history. After 1844 "there should be time no longer" (Revelation 10:6). We no longer have any uncompleted prophetic period predicted in the Word of God. No definite time separates us from the second coming of Christ. The few prophetic details that still await fulfillment could occur within the space of a few weeks.

What really delays the Lord's coming is a task that God wants and is willing to perform in His church today—in every one of us. "Christ is waiting with longing desire for the manifestation of Himself in His church. When the character of Christ shall be perfectly reproduced in His people, then He will come to claim them as His own" (COL 69).

We pause on the verge of eternity. The mighty angel that came down from heaven, setting one foot on the sea and another foot on the earth, and according to Revelation 10 cried with a loud voice and swore by the name of God, assures us that "in the days of the voice of the seventh angel"—our time—"when he shall begin to sound, the mystery of God should be finished" (Revelation 10:7). The everlasting gospel of Jesus will complete its miraculous task in our life and in the world, fully converting the people of God and through the work of the Holy Spirit reaching every nation, language, and people. The end will come, and with it the glorious consummation of the ages. It will arrive whether or not we are prepared.

Satan is trying to distract us so that we will not receive the impressions of the Spirit of God. "The events connected with the close of probation and the work of preparation for the time of trouble, are clearly presented. But multitudes have no more understanding of these important truths than if they had never been revealed. Satan watches to catch away every impression that would make them wise unto salvation, and the time of trouble will find them unready" (GC 594).

May each of us attain the spiritual readiness, and may we have the joy of sharing the glorious victory that Christ is going to give to His people.

Fernando Chaij

Chapter 1

A Panoramic View of Future Events

The Seventh-day Adventist people have in the Bible and in the writings of Ellen G. White an inspired account of the important events of the future, a divine itinerary of its journey toward the City of God. Although it ignores many of the details, inspiration does clearly explain the main features in this challenging trip of ours, and we can see them in a panoramic scenery.

Why Bother With the Negative?

Somebody may ask why we should bother with studying them since they constitute somehow a negative and discouraging aspect of our Christian fight. Is it not better rather to concentrate on the positive facets of our spiritual warfare and enjoy the good and the sunny days God gives us, keeping always a cheerful attitude?

Knowledge of the future according to Bible prophecy and Ellen G. White does not, for two reasons, prevent a real Christian from having a cheerful attitude.

First, God never reveals future trials and tribulations without offering assurance of His never-failing company. Second, such study strengthens the faith and the confidence the child of God has in the loving heavenly Father and wonderful older Brother who trod the pathway of sorrow ahead of us and has assured us, "I am with you alway" (Matthew 28:20).

Satan likes nothing more than the false confidence that results from willful ignorance. He wants us to assume a careless mood and to close our eyes to the strategy he will follow in the spiritual destruction of thousands upon thousands of God's children.

One of the most important points in any warfare is to know the enemy's plans, to explore his capability and power, to become acquainted with the traps, snares, and deceptions he employs. Not only in time of war but even in time of peace armies and states have their spies.

In our Christian warfare "we wrestle not against flesh and blood, but against principalities, against powers, against the rulers of the darkness of this world, against spiritual wickedness in high places" (Ephesians 6:12). And since they are superior to us frail human beings, we desperately need to "put on the whole armour of God" and become fully acquainted with the strategy of so deceptive an enemy. Only then can we avoid defeat and "be able to withstand in the evil day."

"Only those who have been diligent students of the Scriptures and who have received the love of the truth," Mrs. White wrote, "will be shielded from the powerful delusion that takes the world captive. By the Bible testimony these will detect the deceiver in his disguise. To all the testing time will come. By the sifting of temptation the genuine Christian will be revealed." She asks a particularly meaningful question, "Are the people of God now so firmly established upon His word that they would not yield to the evidence of their senses? Would they, in such a crisis, cling to the Bible and the Bible only?" (GC 625).

An Attitude of Spiritual Alertness

We see how important it is for us to remain spiritually alert, remembering our foe's power and astuteness. The

time in which we live requires careful study of the
enemy's devices and plans, a serious consideration of
God's wonderful provisions, and a decided action to
employ all different means of help and aid the Lord has
given us.

"There are in the world today many who close their
eyes to the evidences that Christ has given to warn men
of His coming. They seek to quiet all apprehension,
while at the same time the signs of the end are rapidly
fulfilling, and the world is hastening to the time when
the Son of man shall be revealed in the clouds of heaven"
(AA 260).

The Laodicean stupor takes hold of many minds and
engrosses them in a deceptive attitude of complacency,
making them indifferent to what happens around them.
"Faith in the soon coming of Christ is waning. 'My Lord
delayeth His coming' is not only said in the heart, but
expressed in words and most decidedly in works.
Stupidity in this watching time is sealing the senses of
God's people as to the signs of the times. The terrible
iniquity which abounds calls for the greatest diligence
and for the living testimony, to keep sin out of the
church. Faith has been decreasing to a fearful degree,
and it is only by exercise that it can increase" (3T 255,
256).

Both the Bible and Ellen G. White teach that spiritual
carelessness is not only dangerous but sinful. Particularly, "Paul teaches in 1 Thessalonians 5:4 to 6 that it is
sinful to be indifferent to the signs which are to precede
the second coming of Christ. Those guilty of this neglect
he calls children of the night and of darkness. He encourages the vigilant and watchful with these words: 'But ye,
brethren, are not in darkness, that that day should over-
take you as a thief. Ye are all the children of light, and the
children of the day: we are not of the night, nor of
darkness. Therefore let us not sleep, as do others; but let
us watch and be sober' " (AA 260).

Five Vital Events for the Church

Five great events will deeply affect the church and its members. They are the shaking, the reformation, the sealing, the latter rain, and the finishing of the work of God.

All of them will end at the close of probation and will develop more or less simultaneously. Intimately related, they affect each other. The shaking time will cause some members to leave, while firmly establishing others. Some will participate in the reformation movement quietly going on. Others, clinging to sinful desires and habits, impurity, selfishness, pride, or a struggle for supremacy, will lose the opportunity God gives them to change their lives, purify their souls by the freely imputed righteousness of Christ, and by faith and a real daily surrender to clothe themselves in His imparted righteousness.

So, while some will be receiving the seal of God, others will reject God's leading. Likewise, the outpouring of the Spirit of God in the latter rain will find some fully prepared. And by the power of the Holy Ghost and the convincing lives of those fully converted by the Spirit, thousands upon thousands will quickly accept God's final message. The church's evangelistic task will finish in a blaze of glory. The prophecy of Revelation 18:1 will see its quick fulfillment. All this will happen before the end of probation. The five events will cease abruptly as the investigative judgment ends and the time of trouble begins.

Sometimes we view the shaking process as a future event. But the fact is that we live in the sifting time right now. "I saw that we are now in the shaking time," Mrs. White wrote years ago. "Satan is working with all his power to wrest souls from the hand of Christ and cause them to trample underfoot the Son of God" (1T 429).

And the prophet of God predicted centuries ago,

"Surely in that day there shall be a great shaking in the land of Israel" (Ezekiel 38:19). Although persecution and false teaching will cause the loss of some, the main reason many will leave God's people is their negative reaction to the Laodicean message.

The Meaning of the Shaking

"I asked the meaning of the shaking I had seen and was shown it would be caused by the straight testimony called forth by the counsel of the True Witness to the Laodiceans. This will have its effect upon the heart of the receiver, and will lead him to exalt the standard and pour forth the straight truth. Some will not bear the straight testimony. They will rise up against it, and this is what will cause a shaking among God's people" (EW 270).

What is the essence of that message to Laodicea? It is that you have a totally wrong estimation of your own spiritual condition. You think you need nothing, but the fact is that you are miserable and in desperate straits.

If the Laodicean accepts the verdict from the One who knows our condition much better than we do; if, aroused to his spiritual situation, he repents and seeks forgiveness, accepting the celestial gold of faith and love—fruits of the Holy Spirit—God will completely change his condition. Donning the white robe of the righteousness of Christ and His character, he will not be naked any more. Anointing his eyes with the eyesalve of the Holy Spirit so that he does not continue in blindness but is able to see sin under any disguise, he will triumphantly endure the process of the shaking. Actually he will be forming a character that will receive God's seal.

Going through the growing experience of revival and reformation, he will be among the happy ones baptized by the Holy Spirit, and he will partake in the glorious completion of God's mission on earth.

But if he clings to worldliness, disregarding the loving counsel of repentance and refusing the testimony of those who present the message to Laodicea, not only in words but in their transformed lives, he will accept the "mark of the beast." Finally, sad to say, he will take his place with the lost.

During the Time of Trouble

The shaking, the sealing, the reformation, the latter rain, and the completion of God's work occur simultaneously.

The investigative judgment ends with the reviewing of the names of the living. Heaven issues the decree, "He that is unjust, let him be unjust still; . . . and he that is righteous, let him be righteous still" (Revelation 22:11). Probation ends, and the tremendous time of trouble begins. Only those who have gone through the multiple experience previously referred to will be victorious.

Persecution will have reached its highest peak. Sunday legislation will influence the whole world. God's people will suffer in the prison cells, in the mountains, in the forests, in the deserts. Nevertheless He will shield them from the seven last plagues. The presence of Jesus and the holy angels will make mansions of light and hope of the cells and the dungeons of the righteous. The children of God hiding in the uninhabited places of the earth will receive food, water, and protection by the miraculous intervention of angels.

And when the wicked will stretch their hand, anticipating the day of the death decree, to exterminate from our planet all Sabbathkeepers and to get rid of the hated minority, God will display His power in a mighty manner at midnight. "The sun appears, shining in his strength. Signs and wonders follow in quick succession. The wicked look with terror and amazement upon the scene, while the righteous behold with solemn joy the tokens of their deliverance" (GC 636).

And shortly after different upheavals of nature, the sign of the Son of God appears in heaven, the wicked perish, and the little cloud increases more and more in size until it resolves into Christ surrounded by His holy angels.

Relevant Questions

The last scenes of sinful human history await us. The mighty events predicted in Bible prophecy and enlarged upon in the writings of Ellen White will soon rock the world. The dramatic experiences of the last days will also touch God's church. Are we, as a church and as individuals, fully prepared to meet them? Each one of us should ask himself questions like the following:

Is mine a really deep and meaningful Christian experience, or is it a superficial and formal one?

By a full daily surrender of my heart to God and through a moment-by-moment dependence upon Christ, am I allowing the Holy Spirit to mold my life so that coming events will not sink me into apostasy, desperation, and defeat?

Am I participating in the sealing of God's people? Is the Holy Spirit writing the perfect character of Christ in my heart? Or is any sin or any cherished weakness preventing God from transforming me?

Am I shielding myself with the powerful armor of God so as to be fully prepared to pass through the shaking? Can I stand so that nothing will detach me from God's love even though treason, apostasy, and persecution prevail?

Am I receiving daily the early rain of the Holy Spirit and thus getting ready for the powerful showers of the latter rain?

Am I active enough, witnessing for Christ, so that God can use me in enlightening the whole earth with the last and glorious message of salvation?

Chapter 2

Christ With His Church Through the Ages

When we speak about the true church, we refer to the most wonderful organization that exists in the world. God Himself was its founder, and Jesus is its head. It had its origin early in human history, practically as early as sin made its appearance on our planet. In Genesis 6 we read that humanity began to divide in two different categories, the sons of God and the sons of men.

A Specific Purpose for the Church

Sin kept on widening the gap, since the sons and daughters of men, by opposition to the children of God, separated themselves more and more from God's ideal for the human race. It became necessary for God right there to establish a group of loyal people to preserve His name, His standards of life, and His worship.

Though His special group receives different names in the Bible—chosen people, people of God, Christian church—its main purpose remains the same. It preserves the knowledge of the true God—at first by tradition, and later on by the Written Word. His people represent His character and communicate His message to the rest of the world. At the same time the church in all ages has served as a means of developing human lives fitted for heaven.

"The church is God's appointed agency for the salva-

tion of men," Ellen White wrote. "It was organized for
service, and its mission is to carry the gospel to the
world" (AA 9).

First of all, the church has concern for its own members. Through the different services conducted in it, the
study of the Bible, prayer, Christian fellowship, and the
special presence of God during worship, it unites men
with the Most High, allows the Holy Spirit to speak to
human hearts, and arouses a longing for Christian perfection and a hunger and a thirst for justice. Different
members receive special endowments, the gifts of the
Spirit, "for the perfecting of the saints . . . till we all
come . . . unto a perfect man" (Ephesians 4:12, 13), fully
prepared for heaven.

In addition, God established the church as a missionary agency to carry the gospel to the world, and until it
performs its duty, He cannot consider that it is fulfilling
its main objective.

God has a definite purpose in assigning to His church
such an honorable commission. Our spiritual strength
depends in high degree on our witnessing activity. The
member content with simply knowing a set of teachings,
passively experiencing forgiveness from sin and the
peace and the joy of a direct relationship with God, soon
begins to lose that experience if he does not respond to
the promptings of the Holy Spirit.

"Everyone in whose heart Christ abides, everyone
who will show forth His love to the world, is a worker
together with God for the blessing of humanity. As he
receives from the Saviour grace to impart to others, from
his whole being flows forth the tide of spiritual life" (AA
13).

A High Ideal That Can Be Achieved

Nobody would argue about the high ideal God has
for His church—"a glorious church, not having spot, or

wrinkle; but . . . holy and without blemish" (Ephesians 5:27)—since Paul clearly describes it. The big question in many minds, though: Is it possible to achieve such a high standard? Is such an ideal attainable?

God does not ask for impossibilities. The Word of God abounds in definite assurances: "Whereby are given unto us exceeding great and precious promises: that by these ye might be partakers of the divine nature" (2 Peter 1:4). "Unto him that is able to keep you from falling, and to present you faultless before the presence of his glory with exceeding joy, . . . be glory and majesty, dominion and power" (Jude 24, 25). "Now thanks be unto God, which always causeth us to triumph in Christ, and maketh manifest the savour of his knowledge by us in every place" (2 Corinthians 2:14).

Nevertheless, we must remember that sanctification or perfection is not a fixed level of excellence at which we should aim but a process of continual growth in which we are always progressing toward maturity. At every stage of that process we may be perfect or mature. A baby one year old is perfect at his level if he can take a few steps before falling. At three years he should be able to run without falling, and at sixteen or seventeen he may be quite an athlete. At every one of the three stages his development can be perfect. The child of God can be mature at every level of his growing experience. At every step of the way he may be not only saved by the imputed righteousness of Christ but mature through the work of the Holy Spirit and the process of sanctification and growth.

Naturally it requires constant contact with God, a living, moment-by-moment relationship with Christ. If by a voluntary and continual surrender of his heart and will to God he allows Jesus to live in him and motivate his thoughts, his acts, his feelings, he will find himself growing and achieving maturity, not by any personal merit, but through the action of the Holy Spirit.

We have to remember, though, that God expects a particularly high level of similitude to Christ from the church that lives when probation expires. The last church should and will be without blemish. A historic experience of trials and persecution, along with a special work of the Spirit of God, will make it possible. God fits His people for the seal of God. "Those who receive the seal of the living God and are protected in the time of trouble must reflect the image of Jesus fully" (EW 71). "Not one of us will ever receive the seal of God while our characters have one spot or stain upon them" (5T 214).

Such spiritual maturity, possessed through the grace of God by many individuals through history, will prevail in the church at the time when probation closes. Our cooperation with the power of Heaven allows God to work miracles in us.

But whether it will be my experience or not depends entirely on me.

Surrounded by the Wonderful Love of God

Since it is His institution on earth and has such high objectives, God naturally expresses love and tender regard toward the church. Passages like Zechariah 2:8— "He that toucheth you toucheth the apple of his eye"— eloquently testify to the Lord's affection for His church and the way He identifies with her.

But the church is not a collection of absolutely perfect men and women. Although Scripture calls her members saints and the children of God, they are erring and sinning human beings who are still growing and learning how to live without sin. As mortals they have defects and commit sins and mistakes. Yet "the church, enfeebled and defective though it be, is the only object on earth on which Christ bestows His supreme regard" (2SM 396).

So intimate is Christ's relationship with His church that when John viewed the seven candlesticks—symbol of the church through the ages—he also saw the Son of man among them (Revelation 1:12, 13).

Since God so loves and values the church, no one has the right to attack or do damage to her. Through the centuries there have appeared individuals who, under the guise of zeal for the cause of God, have attacked the church and her organization, causing revolt and destruction.

Any real reform does not attack the church as such or her leaders but will display a spirit of prayer. "The time has come for a thorough reformation to take place. When this reformation begins, the spirit of prayer will actuate every believer and *will banish from the church the spirit of discord and strife*" (8T 251). The fact that somebody downgrades the church, her structure, her leaders, or her doctrines, identifies him as a false reformer, someone misguided, or a fanatic.

Now in considering the love and tender interest of Christ for His church, we should not lose sight of the fact that she consists of members, and the love of God to the body implies His love for every individual that belongs to her. The thought of Jesus' keen personal interest, patience, and tender care for every one of us, especially when we go through trials, difficulties, and tribulations, or when we have sinned but return to the Lord with contrite hearts and repentance, should comfort every one of us.

The Church, Now Militant, Will Become Triumphant

The symbol of a mighty army is one of the most appropriate illustrations to depict God's church. With Christ as its Commander in chief (Song of Solomon 6:10; Matthew 28:18-20), it vanquishes the evil enemy.

The church must meet three conditions for victory. First, she must always actively do the job assigned to her: the witnessing program and the evangelistic task.

Second, she must keep her eyes on the Author and Con-summator of our faith, the One who assured us, "I am with you alway, even unto the end of the world." In other words, the church must have a close unity with Him, depending on His power, His promises, and the working of His Spirit.

In her aggressive program of evangelization the church will confront trials, obstacles, hardships, and persecution. It happened in the past and will reoccur in the future, especially in the dark days when apostate powers confederate against God and His people.

Speaking of the disciples, E. G. White wrote that "only as they were united with Christ could the disciples hope to have the accompanying power of the Holy Spirit and the co-operation of angels of heaven. . . . So long as they remained united, the church would go forth 'fair as the moon, clear as the sun, and terrible as an army with banners.' (Song of Solomon 6:10). Nothing could with-stand her onward progress. The church would advance from victory to victory, gloriously fulfilling her divine mission of proclaiming the gospel to the world" (AA 90, 91).

The third factor in the success of the church is whether she reflects the character of Christ. "The church illuminates the world, not by their profession of godli-ness, but by their manifestation of the transforming, sanctifying power of the truth on life and character" (1SM 133).

Am I active? Am I united with Christ and depending on Him? Do I reflect the excellency of His character, showing the transforming power of His truth?

God has promised to finish the church's task. Al-though it may seem today an impossible mission, God has ample power and means to fulfill His word. And He does not lie. "This gospel of the kingdom *shall be preached* in all the world" (Matthew 24:14). The mighty angel that came down from heaven in Revelation 10, after embracing the earth and the sea and lifting up his hand to swear by the One who lives forever, said, "In the days of the voice of the seventh angel, when he shall begin to sound, *the mystery of God* [the proclamation of the gospel] *should be finished,* as he has declared to his servants the prophets" (Revelation 10:7). The divine statements leave no shadow of doubt. They are both prophecies and promises.

God's church succeeds, not through its own strength, but through the power of the Holy Spirit, since the Lord of hosts says, "not by might, nor by power, but by my spirit" (Zechariah 4:6).

Am I a consecrated part of a church that has such a glorious mission? Am I taking advantage of my opportunities and participating in its witnessing program?

A Change of Scene

The devoted, active, and militant church—engaged in an aggressive task of communicating the gospel to the whole world, facing the rage of an enemy who knows that he has but a short time—soon will become the victorious, triumphant church of God. She will fight her final battles against the great threefold alliance of powers directed by Satan and united with the political states. They will have law and its enforcement agencies on their side. The future will seem hopeless.

But on the night that the Lord intervenes to liberate His people, the scene changes completely. The persecuted minority will witness the destruction of the evil forces and the miraculous manifestation of God's power.

And shortly after that, when Christ resurrects those who sleep in the grave to join the transformed living saints, all the redeemed together will constitute the triumphant church. The final church of all ages marches on to receive its great reward. It is then when the jubilant scene described in Revelation 7:9 and 10 happens. "After this I beheld, and, lo, a great multitude, which no man could number, of all nations, and kindreds, and people, and tongues, stood before the throne, and before the Lamb, clothed with white robes, and palms in their hands; and cried with a loud voice, saying, Salvation to our God which sitteth upon the throne, and unto the Lamb."

"If the church will put on the robe of Christ's righteousness, withdrawing from all allegiance with the world," Mrs. White stated, "there is before her the dawn of a bright and glorious day. God's promise to her will stand fast forever. He will make her an eternal excellency, a joy of many generations. . . . Endowed with divine energy, it will cut its way through the strongest barriers and triumph over every obstacle" (AA 601).

And after the task is done, we partake of the exceeding joy of the redeemed, of being a part of the church triumphant. May God give us this experience as a result of our loyalty to Him.

The Main Reason Behind the Success

The main reason for the eternal success of the church is that Jesus Himself is her head and her foundation. Establishing her Himself, He designed her work and her program. He promised and gave her power through the ages, especially during the last hour of strife and darkness. Therefore, no matter how hard her task, nothing can defeat her because He has all power in heaven and in earth.

The strength of a building depends in great measure on the quality of foundation it has. Civil engineers take great care to calculate the kind and type of foundation a building needs. Years ago a firm erected a fifteen-story building in the city of Buenos Aires. When the construction company began the final details, the unexpected happened one noon. Tragedy struck. The whole building collapsed, killing several workers and wounding many. Immediately the builders looked for the engineer in charge of the work. But they could not find him. Knowing that, in order to save money, he had not laid the right foundation for that big complex, he had fled the country. He realized that he would be made responsible for the tragedy and the loss.

Thank God for the assurance we have that the foundation of the church will resist the trial of time, because it is the Rock of Ages.

The other illustration the Bible uses to describe the relationship of Jesus Christ with His church is equally meaningful: "He [Christ] is the head of the body" (Colossians 1:18). The connection of the head with every part of the body is absolutely vital. An accident resulting in brain or spinal damage could affect any function of any member. It could paralyze part or even the whole of the body.

Another thought the symbol of a body brings us is that when one member suffers pain, the whole organism is in distress. So in the church "we, being many, are one body in Christ, and every one members one of another" (Romans 12:5).

On the other hand, if Christ is the head and the bigger Brother of all of us, and God is the heavenly Father of all, we are mutually related as brothers and sisters. Our feelings and affections are those of brothers and sisters related by birth, and the love that connects us to Christ and to God unites us in an unbreakable bond.

Chapter 3

Persecution and the Christian

The fact of persecution and trial in the life of the Christian poses one of the human mind's puzzling problems: Why is it necessary that suffering and pain be always a part of the experience of the child of God? And why is it that such a powerful God, a tender Father, full of love, should allow His creatures to go through the agony of physical and moral suffering when He is completely able to deliver them?

When Peter started to refuse to let the Master wash his feet, Jesus told him, "What I do thou knowest not now" (John 13:7). We are not in a position to understand in the present world all of God's reasons for permitting something. His wisdom is infinite, whereas our mind, our understanding, and our experience are finite. Just as we cannot expect to contain the whole sea in a glass, so we cannot grasp God's ways by our limited minds. Thus we need to exercise faith and accept what God allows to happen in our life as best for us.

But on the other hand, God does not want our faith to be a blind one. Within the reach of our understanding we have enough facts to give our faith a firm foundation and to make ours a "reasonable service" (Romans 12:1). We have enough promises, experiences, and explanations to let us fully trust in the wisdom and the love of our heavenly Father.

The Blessed Purpose of Trials and Persecution

The following list suggests some of the benefits of trials and persecutions in the life of a Christian.

1. Trials and hardship strengthen our faith in God, since faith, like muscles, increases through exercise. Think of what happened in the lives of Job, Joseph, and Paul, and in the blessed results of their vicissitudes.

2. They produce a state of mind in which we are more prone to pray. Thus they open for us the door of communication with Heaven and make it more possible for God to convey to our hearts the message we need.

3. They cause us to examine our lives, to ponder our spiritual needs and character defects, and to ask God if some personal sin or mistake caused the tribulation. Does anything in me prevent God from blessing or intervening for my success? What does the Holy Spirit want to teach me through the experience?

4. They prepare our character for heaven. "No cross, no crown," wrote Ellen White. "How can one be strong in the Lord without trials? To have strength we must exercise. . . . It is through much tribulation that we are to enter the kingdom of God" (3T 67).

   a. Difficulties cleanse us from selfishness. "Often we enter the furnace of trial with our souls darkened with selfishness; but if patient under the crucial test, we shall come forth reflecting the divine character" (COL 175).

   b. They remove character defects. "You need not be surprised if with hammer and chisel God cuts away the sharp corners of your character until you are prepared to fill the place He has for you. No human being can accomplish this work. Only by God can it be done. And be assured that He will not strike one useless blow" (7T 264).

   c. Hardships defeat self-trust and show the self-sufficient their helplessness. "Everyone has **undiscov-**

ered traits of character that must come to light through trial. God allows those who are self-sufficient to be sorely tempted, that they may understand their helplessness" (7T 210, 211).

d. Trials enable us to receive from Him renewed strength and increased humility. "When trials and tribulations come to you know that they are sent in order that you may receive from the Lord of glory renewed strength and increased humility, so that He may safely bless and support and uphold you" (ML 185).

"We miss very much because we do not grasp the blessings that may be ours in our afflictions. All our sufferings and sorrows, all our temptations and trials, all our sadness and griefs, all our persecutions and privations, and in short all things, work together for our good. . . . All experiences and circumstances are God's workmen whereby good is brought to us. Let us look at the light behind the cloud" (ML 185).

e. They purify us and prepare us to receive the seal of God. "I saw that those who of late have embraced the truth would have to know what it is to suffer for Christ's sake, that they would have trials to pass through that would be keen and cutting, in order that they may be purified and fitted through suffering to receive the seal of the living God, pass through the time of trouble, see the King in His beauty, and dwell in the presence of God and pure, holy angels" (EW 67).

f. Problems should teach us to be tolerant of others that suffer. "But this experience [great agitation and trial] was just what they needed to teach them forbearance toward others in a similar state of trial" (2T 20).

5. They enable us to understand and help others who face tribulation. "Blessed be God . . . who comforteth us in all our tribulation, that we may be able to comfort them which are in any trouble, by the comfort wherewith we ourselves are comforted of God" (2 Corinthians 1:3, 4).

Persecution in the Past

One of the most encouraging blessings Christ pro-
nounced in His Sermon on the Mount was, "Blessed are
they that mourn: for they shall be comforted" (Matthew
5:4). He does not specify the reason for the mourning.
Whatever the kind of trial, He calls those that mourn
blessed and promises them comfort. It affects those who
reap what they have sown, even those who weep because of their own sins. If they are sad, if they suffer, God
stretches His hand out to uphold them.

But if Christ's blessing applies to one kind of tribulation more than any other, it is persecution. He refers to it
in Matthew 10:16-25: "Behold, I send you forth as sheep
in the midst of wolves. . . . They will deliver you up to
the councils, and they will scourge you in their
synagogues; and ye shall be brought before governors
and kings for my sake."

God's promises that assure His children of His care
and love, especially during persecution, do not imply
that He will always protect them from suffering or deliver them from death. Millions of martyrs lost their lives
during the fierce persecutions of the Roman Empire and
during the terrible ordeals of the Middle Ages and afterward. But the more Satan instigated humanity to impose
suffering and death on the Christians, the more their
wonderful and courageous testimony won new hearts,
convinced new minds, and caused the kingdom of God
to prosper. As a result, Satan changed his tactics and
began to corrupt the church by other means. He gave her
popularity, full freedom, the official favor of the government, and finally united her with the state.

But whenever oppression occurred it kept the church
growing spiritually and numerically. And in spite of
relatively peaceful times, "till the close of time there will
be a conflict between the church of God and those who
are under the control of evil angels" (AA 219).

The strength of the church and her effectiveness in witnessing for Christ reached a peak during apostolic times and immediately afterward, when the church faced difficult times. She preached the gospel in the then known world and even made an inroad in the imperial palace.

Persecution in the Last Days

But persecution is not only a matter of history. Right now countries exist where the children of God have to work under difficult conditions. Restrictions and oppression will soon become global, according to Bible prophecy.

The beast with two horns like a lamb of Revelation 13: 11 to 14, the great country that up to now has fulfilled a blessed historic mission by being a stronghold of freedom and religious liberty, in the near future will speak as a dragon. Transforming itself into a persecuting power, it will unite itself with the first beast of Revelation 13, Rome, to impose obligatory Sunday religious observance in violation of the fourth commandment and to require allegiance to religious dogmas that are in conflict with the Word of God.

To those who decide to be loyal to God instead of to man it will deny even the most elemental constitutional rights. They will not have the right to work under normal conditions or to buy and sell. Eventually they will have to abandon the populated cities and crowded areas, where life will be impossible for them and where they would be the target of boycott.

Nevertheless, despite hard circumstances they will have to finish the church's task. The church must acquaint the great cities and the whole world with the truth about God so that everyone can intelligently make a decision. Most probably some may lose their life, many will suffer affliction, and we will see the history of martyrdom renewed once again, although not to the extent of the Middle Ages.

After the close of probation the toils and trials will be even greater. The human governments will issue a death decree against Sabbathkeepers (Revelation 13:15). But we have the assurance that no martyrs will die during the time of trouble: "If the righteous were now [during the time of trouble] left to fall a prey to their enemies, it would be a triumph for the prince of darkness" (GC 634). "So I saw that the people of God, who had faithfully warned the world of His coming wrath, would be delivered. God would not suffer the wicked to destroy those who were expecting translation and who would not bow to the decree of the beast to receive his mark" (EW 284).

Now is the time for us to develop in our character the elements of strength, courage, faith in God, and absolute dependence on Him so that such events do not take us unaware. It is time to cultivate a relationship so close with the Lord that we will naturally remain loyal to Him in perplexing circumstances.

God's Concept About His Persecuted Children

God does not remain passive or uninterested during the church's fierce battle against the powers of darkness. First of all, let's remember that Christ already has won the battle for us, and from then on Satan has been a defeated enemy, bound to destruction. Christ's victory during His life and on the cross not only assures ours but makes God vitally concerned about our fight. More than that, He is aggressively involved in it and provides us with everything we need to triumph.

During our terrible struggle He offers us the heavenly panoply. "Be strong in the Lord, and in the power of his might. Put on the whole armour of God, that ye may be able to stand against the wiles of the devil" (Ephesians 6:10, 11). Speaking of spiritual armor, Paul assures us of its absolute effectiveness. "The weapons of our warfare are not carnal, but mighty through God to the pulling down of strong holds" (2 Corinthians 10:4). No matter how solid are his strongholds, no matter what devices the enemy uses, the weapons God puts at our disposal are mightier and more effective.

We do not fight alone. Jesus pronounces a blessing on His persecuted children, especially the ones afflicted for His sake (Matthew 5:10-12). And if God considers us blessed, we have no reason for any fear or defeat. To the contrary, we should "rejoice, and be exceeding glad: for great is . . . [our] reward in heaven."

When we remember that God watches over us, we can know that no temptation, no affliction, will prove greater than we, with His help, can endure. With every temptation He mercifully gives us a way out. It should prompt us to go forth with courage and faith.

Victory: the Great Christian Word

In the Christian vocabulary *victory* is the great word. It is not merely a philosophical concept, a wishful thinking, or a vague possibility. Rather, it is an absolute reality. As John watched the prophetic screen with eager interest to see what would happen after the conflict between good and evil ended he saw something that filled his heart with joy and praises.

"I beheld, and, lo, a great multitude, which no man could number, of all nations, and kindreds, and people, and tongues, stood before the throne, and before the Lamb, clothed with white robes, and palms in their hands; and cried with a loud voice, saying, Salvation to our God which sitteth upon the throne, and unto the Lamb. And all the angels stood round about the throne, and about the elders and the four beasts, and fell before the throne on their faces, and worshipped God" (Revelation 7:9-11).

They are the victorious. When one of the elders asked, "What are these which are arrayed in white robes? and whence come they?" the revelator answered, "Sir, thou knowest. And he [the same elder] said to me, These are they which came out of great tribulation, and have washed their robes, and made them white in the blood of the Lamb" (verses 13, 14). In other words, they are the redeemed who in life went through persecution, affliction, and tribulation. Every one of them is a living testimony that in Christ our victory is assured.

The ones that lived during the last days, who have gone through a particularly fierce battle against Satan and refused to submit to the beast, express their great gladness with a special song. "They sing the song of Moses the servant of God, and the song of the Lamb" (Revelation 15:3). It is a song of victory and praise to God for their great salvation.

"When God was about to open to the beloved John the history of the church for future ages, He gave him an assurance of the Saviour's interest and care for His people by revealing to him 'One like unto the Son of man,' walking among the candlesticks, which symbolized the seven churches. While John was shown the last great struggles of the church with earthly powers, he was also permitted to behold the final victory and deliverance of the faithful. He saw the church brought into deadly conflict with the beast and his image, and the worship of that beast enforced on pain of death. But looking beyond the smoke and din of the battle, he beheld a company upon Mount Zion with the Lamb, having, instead of the mark of the beast, the 'Father's name written in their foreheads.' And again he saw 'them that had gotten the victory over the beast, and over his image, and over his mark, and over the number of his name, stand on the sea of glass, having the harps of God' and singing the song of Moses and the Lamb" (5T 752, 753).

The Source of Our Victory

As we already stated, the only source of victory in our Christian life is Christ, His sacrifice, His righteousness, His power, His indwelling presence in our heart. In Revelation 12:11 the apostle says, "They [the persecuted people of God] overcame him [the dragon: Satan and all his representatives and instruments] by the blood of the Lamb."

Christ is the only basis for our redemption. The blood of the Lamb is effective not only for the forgiveness of sin but also for its conquering and eradication. In the name of that blood spilled for us we can claim, at every step of the way, the promise of victory.

Jesus left us the certainty that "whatsoever ye shall ask in my name, that will I do, that the Father may be glorified in the Son" (John 14:13). We know it is God's will that we have victory over sin, temptation, and tribulation; steadfastness and courage in time of trouble; and loyalty during persecution and threat of death. Since Jesus has committed Himself and promised that if we ask something in His name, the Father will grant it, we can, with absolute faith, boldly take that wonderful promise in moments of need.

That means that we have at the same time to learn how to be in constant contact with Him through the study of His Word, through prayer and meditation, and through a continual surrender to Him. These are the means God uses to mold our life and impress in our heart His divine character.

But Revelation 12:11 adds still another dimension. Christians overcome the devil not only by appropriating the merits of "the blood of the Lamb" but also "by the word of their testimony." We testify in favor of Christ and His truth not only through our words as we use every opportunity to witness for our Redeemer and for what He has done for us but also through our life—a life consistent with what we profess. It takes both aspects.

Each of us has a circle of people with whom we come into daily contact in our neighborhood or business. Our testimony outwardly expresses our faith in Jesus. Giving it strengthens and develops our Christian experience, reaffirms our trust in God, and invigorates our relationship with Him.

Chapter 4

Symbols of Apostate
Persecuting Powers

One of the Bible's most amazing and convincing features is prophecy. Fulfillment of prophecy offers objective evidence of the divine inspiration of the Word. And Scripture predicts definite periods of persecution centuries beforehand.

The different elements used by the Bible as symbols of powers that would persecute the church and the truth correspond so well with the historic reality that no one studying them should have any doubt regarding their identification and what the future has in store for us.

Years ago, when I was a young university student, I took an oral examination before an examining board. One of its members was a famous humanist who was a great scholar but a staunch agnostic. The subjects that I had to speak about included philosophy of history. Before long I had the opportunity of referring to the Christian philosophy of history, namely, that God leads in the great movements of history. In order to illustrate the position, I explained with a diagram on the blackboard the amazing fulfillment of the seventy-week prophecy. While my own teacher, who was one of the members, evidently seemed happy with the exposition, it enraged the agnostic teacher. After I finished that part of my dissertation, he began denying any validity to Bible prophecy.

But being himself a great historian he could not deny the correspondence of historic fulfillment with Bible prediction. So, in order to reject inspiration, he needed to deny the authenticity of the Book of Daniel. It is not possible anymore, though, to refuse the historicity and authenticity of Daniel or of any other prophetic portion of the Bible. We know that the Biblical authors wrote down their predictions long before the events began to happen. And these predictions offer a convincing testimony that God has divinely inspired the Good Book.

But what should especially encourage the Bible student is the bright outcome, the wonderful finale, of Satan's warfare against God and His children. The enemy now strikes his final desperate blows like a drowning man in his last struggles.

Let us keep in mind the final scene of victory. Maintaining our eyes on our Invincible Captain, who never lost a single battle, we must always remember that He will be with us. The voice of Jesus resounds across the centuries to bring us the same message of strength He sent to the church of Ephesus: "I know thy works, and tribulation. . . . Fear none of those things which thou shalt suffer: behold, the devil shall cast some of you into prison, that ye may be tried; and ye shall have tribulation: . . . be thou faithful unto death, and I will give thee a crown of life" (Revelation 2:9, 10).

The Dragon

The first great symbol that appears in Revelation is the red dragon. Being Satan himself (Revelation 12:9), he also symbolizes several instruments he employs, namely, the different universal kingdoms that afflicted the people of God, especially the Roman Empire (verses 3, 4). Also the dragon represents Romanism and the Papacy during the 1260 years (verses 6, 14). The same dragon will direct the last period of persecution against

the remnant church (verse 17). In Revelation 16:13 the
dragon as well depicts spiritualism and the occult mixed
with Christianity.

The actions of the pagan kingdoms, the methods
used by the Roman Church, and the manifestations of
the occult all have a common denominator—the power of
Satan. That is why Scripture presents all the different
aspects of persecution as being unlashed by the same
power: the dragon. The earthly powers championed Satan's cause, and he uses them.

Revelation 12:9 says that the dragon was "*cast out*
[from heaven] *into the earth.*" One could apply the passage to different moments of Satan's history.

First, to the moment the sin of Lucifer became unpar-
donable. Before the creation of man, he rejected the
efforts of God and the loyal angels to draw him to repentance. Heaven, after a tremendous battle, cast the devil
with his angels down to earth (Revelation 12:7-9; PP
35-42; EW 145, 146).

Second, to the Crucifixion. Until then, with some
restrictions, he could contact the angels, but he did not
live in heaven anymore. Christ said of that moment,
"Now shall the prince of this world be cast out" (John
12:31). Revelation 12:9 mainly refers to this second event
for the following verse alludes to Christ's victory at the
cross: "Now is come salvation, and strength, and the
kingdom of our God, and the power of his Christ" (verse
10).

"When Satan became fully conscious that there was
no possibility of his being brought again into favor with
God, his malice and hatred began to be manifest" (EW
146). His hostility, which began after his first expulsion
from heaven, intensified even more after Calvary. When
the prophet saw him, he exclaimed, "Woe to the in-
habiters of the earth and of the sea! for the devil is come
down unto you, having great wrath, because he
knoweth that he hath but a short time" (Revelation

12:12). He knows that he is already defeated and doomed to destruction. We should rejoice in that certainty.

The Beast of Seven Heads and Ten Horns

In a sense the first beast of Revelation 13 is similar to the dragon of Revelation 12. Evidently the seven heads are the same as in Revelation 12:3. It is easier to find out what kingdoms the heads represented when we read 13:2, because it ties the prophecy with Daniel 7, where the lion represents Babylon, the bear Medo-Persia, and the leopard the Hellenistic empire of Alexander the Great. So it is logical to conclude that both here and in chapter 12 the seven heads symbolize seven successive kingdoms that afflict God's people. The total list could be Egypt, Assyria, Babylon, Medo-Persia, the Hellenistic Greece, pagan Rome, and papal Rome. It is a continuous, historic process of enmity against God. All of them, especially the last one, received power and authority from the dragon, who is primarily Satan (verse 2).

If it is true that the multiple symbol stands for an uninterrupted succession of persecuting powers, it is also evident that John referred particularly to the last head, papal Rome. Here the prophet uses the resource of a synecdoche to present the whole historic background, but pointing to one outstanding element. It becomes clear when we read and analyze the entire description of the beast.

The ten horns indicate the geographical area or territory, both here and in chapter 12, namely, the divided Europe during the Middle Ages. In chapter 13 the Revelator looks at the scenes more from the religious angle, whereas in chapter 12 the point of view is a political one. So in both cases we deal with the same powers, the same territory, and the same period, but with different insights.

The beast's tremendous acts (blasphemy, great

words, and persecution) and the period in which that persecution occurs (forty-two months as compared with three and a half years in Daniel) identify it with the papal Rome of Daniel 7.

When do the 1260 years begin and end? In 533 the emperor of the Eastern Roman Empire, Justinian I, promulgated a decree establishing that the bishop of Rome was the supreme hierarch of Christendom. When Belisarius, his general, finished his victorious career of conquest against the Arian Ostrogoths of Italy in 538, he enforced the decree. It gave a religious and political supremacy to the pope.

Starting from the two dates—533 and 538—and adding the 1260 years, we arrive at the end of the prophetic period, the years 1793 and 1798. What happened during them, and what historic process was then taking place?

In 1793 France caught the attention of the Western world. Four years earlier the French Revolution had begun. The revolutionist leaders were decidedly anti-Catholic and atheistic. Finally, in 1793, the new government launched a fierce attack against the Roman Church. The revolutionists enthroned the goddess Reason, depriving the priests of their religious status, and an antichurch campaign proclaimed "that no other national worship should exist other than the national worship of Liberty and Holy Equality" (Ch. Seignobos, *Historia Universal*, Vol. 5, p. 411).

And 1798 is the year in which the French general Berthier entered the city of Rome to proclaim a republic, took in custody the Roman pontiff, and stripped him of his privileges and political authority. A few years after that the pope lost his territories. Thus the seventh head, the Papacy as an institution, received a wound of death (verse 3). But according to the same verse that head would begin to be healed. The healing became evident when Mussolini signed a concordat with the pope in 1929.

The seventh head, in the process of healing, makes all the world wonder after the beast (Revelation 13:3).

The Lamblike Beast

We will not repeat here the reasons we identify the second beast of Revelation 13 with the United States except to say that they involve the beast's time of appearance, the geographical area, and the country's characteristics while the beast behaved as a lamb.

We want to present here additional insights that describe more fully how the actions of the second beast lead to an allegiance of the civil powers to Rome and to Satan. It centers around the keeping of a false day of rest. Verse 12 says that "he exerciseth all the power of the first beast [Rome] before him, and causeth the earth . . . to worship the first beast." Evidently the government of the United States will dictate laws imposing religious practices. Complying with them would mean an acknowledgment of the first beast's authority.

If we compare the passage with the message of the third angel of Revelation 14:9, 10, we can see clearly that the worship of the (first) beast consists in taking the mark of the beast, which in essence is Sunday observance. So the expression "causeth the earth . . . to worship the . . . beast" is equivalent to "obligates the people to comply with Sunday observance." All those who accept it render allegiance to Rome, thus getting the mark of the beast. In contrast, the true people of God, who "keep the commandments of God" (Revelation 14:12), receive the seal of the living God.

Another reason that leads us to conclude that the worship of Rome has to do with the day of rest is that the little horn—the first beast of Revelation 13—"shall . . . think to change times and laws" (Daniel 7:25). And history demonstrates that the Roman church tried to alter the only commandment that speaks about times, the fourth. So any enactment requiring from the people Sunday observance would cause them to worship the beast and to give obedience to an apostate power instead of God. Thus a spirit of intolerance and persecution will arise in the heart of the nation that up to then was a stronghold of civil and religious freedom.

The other aspect of the prophecy announces, "to them that dwell on the earth, that they should make an image to the [first] beast" (verse 14), that is to say, Rome. For the people to make an image of the beast would be equivalent to shaping a religious structure that controls the power of the state, using it to impose religious observances, as was the case with the medieval church. It is an unholy fusion that puts the church under the state and obligates it to force religious practices on the people, with grave penalties for those that resist.

What Is the Image of the Beast?

It should be a religiopolitical structure similar to Rome, the original beast: a church or a conglomerate of churches united for persecuting purposes, using the civil powers to make a certain form of religion mandatory. Ellen White wrote that "when the Protestant churches shall unite with the secular power to sustain a false religion, for opposing which their ancestors endured the fiercest persecution; when the state shall use its power to enforce the decrees and sustain the institutions of the church—then will Protestant America have formed an image to the papacy, and there will be a national apostasy which will end only in national ruin" (7BC 976).

The Mark of the Beast

As the sign, the mark, or the seal of God, placed by the Holy Spirit on the true children of God reveals itself outwardly in a visible and public manifestation—the observance of the seventh day—the mark of the beast has to do with a false day of rest, Sunday. The seal of God implies absolute obedience to the law of God as a recognition of His supreme authority and love, while the mark of the beast denotes submission to an apostate power, the antichrist, and to Satan, from whom it receives power and authority.

In spite of the fact that it will be decreed necessary to have the mark of the beast to be able to subsist, to buy and sell, to work, and to escape the intended consequences of the death decree (verses 15, 17), some will not accept it either in the right hand or in the forehead, neither by sheer official obligation nor by mental conviction. The courageous minority made up by the true people of God will refuse to bow down before Rome, the state, the popular confederated churches, and Satan. They have their eyes on Christ and proclaim perfect allegiance to God.

In that dark hour that will envelop the world, God's children will leave the populated centers. At the enactment of the federal Sunday laws, which will be imitated by the other countries of the world, the loyal people of God will abandon the great cities and will establish themselves in the countryside or in small towns. After the close of probation, when the authorities issue the death decree, they will flee even from the small localities. Some will face imprisonment; others will flee to live in caves, mountains, deserts, and other isolated places. There the power of God and the ministry of angels will sustain them (EW 282).

The mark of the beast has not yet been imposed, though, nor will it be until every person has had the opportunity of knowing the significance of Sabbath observance. Each individual must come to realize that the Sabbath leads him (1) to recognize God as the Creator and commemorates His work of Creation (Genesis 2:2, 3;

Exodus 20:8-11); (2) to accept the Sabbath as a sign of the sanctification God performs in the human heart (Exodus 31:13; 1 Thessalonians 4:3; 2 Thessalonians 3:13); (3) to acknowledge Jesus as the Lord of the Sabbath and as the Author of the new creation (Mark 2:28; 2 Corinthians 4:17); and (4) to remember the holy day as a sign of man's rest from works of sin and of his entering into the rest of the heart that Jesus promises to those who follow Him (Hebrews 4:1-10).

"There are many who have never had the light. They are deceived by their teachers, and they have not received the mark of the beast. The Lord is working with them; He has not left them to their own ways. Until they shall be convicted of the truth, and trample upon the evidence given to enlighten them, the Lord will not withdraw His grace from them" (EGW, 7BC 976).

"No one has yet received the mark of the beast. . . . There are true Christians in every church, not excepting the Roman Catholic communion. None are condemned until they have had the light and have seen the obligation of the fourth commandment. But when the decree shall go forth enforcing the counterfeit sabbath, and the loud cry of the third angel shall warn men against the worship of the beast and his image, the line will be clearly drawn between the false and the true. Then those who still continue in transgression will receive the mark of the beast" (Ev 234, 235).

A Quadruple Union

Actually Revelation 16:13 speaks of three allied powers conducting an unholy warfare against the church and the truth: *the dragon,* here impersonating spiritualism and the occult, not only in Christian countries but also in pagan environments; *the beast,* Rome, the Papacy; *the false prophet,* which is none other than the image of the beast of Revelation 13, namely apostate Protestantism.

But since in Revelation 13:14 the image of the beast involves a church united to a state—we can well think of a quadruple union.

From a human standpoint it is apparently invincible. The political states with their laws and their armies have united with the ideological and spiritual forces. Behind all four stands the mastermind of the fallen cherubim, the archenemy of God, making his last desperate effort as he realizes that he has but a short time.

Revelation 16:13, 14, reveals the unity, the origin, and the intention of their fierce attack. From the mouth of every one of the three symbols comes out an unclean spirit. They are "spirits of devils, working miracles, which go forth unto the kings of the earth and of the whole world, to gather them to the battle" of Armageddon. Satan marshals them to go to all the world, wielding it together for the last struggle between good and evil.

Revelation 13:13 states that the United States, already in union with Romanism and Protestantism, and with the aid of spiritualism, works great wonders, even making fire come down from heaven, thus convincing the world of the movement's divine origin. The infiltration of modern spiritualism in Protestant churches, the appearance of miracles both in Catholic and Protestant circles, and the strange and new happenings that we will see in the near future will seem so convincing that most will consider them undeniable. Agnostic scientists that up to then rejected the idea of any supernatural force will test the phenomena. When such signs begin to happen they will be forced to accept their reality and will go a step further—they will accept them as of divine origin.

The Bright Outcome of an Agelong Conflict

In Revelation 19:11-21 we have a vivid description of the great finale of the cosmic drama. We see the armies of the Lord, commanded by Jesus, destroying those of the devil. Next we watch the beast, the kings of the earth that afflicted the people of God, their armies, the false prophet and all those who worshiped his image, cast alive into the lake of fire. The lake will destroy the evil ones and cleanse the earth, preparing it to be the beautiful home of the redeemed (verses 19, 20).

The triumph of God and His people should also be ours. We can so identify with God, our Father, and with Jesus, our Master and Lord, that in that day of joy we shall be a part of that eternal victory.

No matter how much we may suffer and endure persecution, with Paul we may exclaim, "I have fought a good fight, I have finished my course, I have kept the faith: henceforth there is laid up for me a crown of righteousness, which the Lord, the righteous judge, shall give me at that day: and not to me only, but unto all them also that love his appearing" (2 Timothy 4:7, 8).

Chapter 5

The Time of Trouble, Part 1

The "time of trouble" will be a unique experience for all the living saints. So much so that the Word of God, in referring to it, says, "There shall be a time of trouble, such as never was since there was a nation even to that same time" (Daniel 12:1). If the prophet, by divine inspiration, explains that it will be without comparison because of the gravity and the seriousness of the events that take place during its span, we had better heed his words and try to learn as much as possible about it. But more than that, our most urgent need is to acquire the necessary preparation for it so that we will not then find ourselves outside the circle of God's protection.

Actually the people of God, by and large, will find that once they begin to go through the ordeal, the trouble will be greater than they ever anticipated. "It is often the case that trouble is greater in anticipation than in reality," wrote Ellen White; "but this is not true of the crisis before us. The most vivid presentation cannot reach the magnitude of the ordeal" (GC 622). The worst part is that, according to the same inspired writer, "we shall need an experience which we do not now possess and which many are too indolent to obtain" (GC 622).

What transpires during the time of trouble will have no previous parallel. But more than that, its importance resides in the fact that we find ourselves personally involved in the crisis. Hence, we must know the kind of readiness we must have in order to go through it triumphantly. Also we need to know how to acquire this readiness and when.

The seriousness of the experience is so great, Mrs. White assures that "many [believers] will be laid away to sleep before the fiery ordeal of the time of trouble shall come upon our world" (CH 375) and also that the same will happen with many children. "The Lord has often instructed me that many little ones are to be laid away before the time of trouble" (CG 566). God will not submit any one of us or any family to a trial greater than what we can bear with His help.

The Time: Beginning and End

Fortunately we are told that the span of the time of trouble, although unknown, will be short (1T 204); also that God reduces it for the sake of the redeemed (GC 631). It begins when Christ leaves the sanctuary, bringing to an end His intercessory work. The people of God, by the power of the Holy Spirit given to them as a consequence of the latter-rain experience, have finished their task in the world. Jesus lifts His hands and exclaims, "It is done," and all the angels of heaven throw their crowns at His feet. Then Heaven will issue the decree, "He that is unjust, let him be unjust still: and he which is filthy, let him be filthy still: and he that is righteous, let him be righteous still: and he that is holy, let him be holy still" (Revelation 22:11; see GC 613, 614; PP 201).

Another event unseen by human eyes will happen to unleash the time of trouble: the letting loose, at the command of God, of the four angels that hold back the symbolic winds of strife and human passion. "Four mighty angels hold back the powers of this earth till the servants of God are sealed in their foreheads. The nations of the world are eager for conflict; but they are held in check by the angels. When this restraining power is removed, there will come a time of trouble and anguish. Deadly instruments of warfare will be invented. Vessels, with their living cargo, will be entombed in the great deep. All who have not the spirit of truth will unite under the leadership of satanic agencies" (7BC 967).

The moment of trial for the redeemed ends when God intervenes to deliver His own with the dramatic manifestation of His mighty power. At midnight the sun unexpectedly shines and the voice of God resounds from heaven with majestic tones (EW 35; GC 636, 637).

Jacob's Dramatic Experience

The falling of the seven last plagues will enrage the wicked. In their deceived imaginations they will consider the small minority of Sabbathkeepers responsible for the judgments of God, and they will issue a death decree against them, to eradicate them from the earth at one stroke (EW 36, 37).

From that hour on, at least after the second plague pours out on the earth, the situation will worsen for the saints. Many will face imprisonment. Some will flee to the mountains and other desolate places (GC 626).

The special period that extends from the moment of the decree's enactment until the liberation hour we call the time of Jacob's trial because it resembles the ancient patriarch's dramatic experience.

Genesis 32:22-30 briefly relates the intensely human episode of Jacob's life, and Ellen White adds fascinating details to it in the description that appears in *Patriarchs and Prophets* (pp. 197-203).

That memorable night, Jacob, having sent his people ahead to a safe place, stayed alone in a solitary, mountainous, and dangerous site by the brook Jabbok to plead with the Lord. "Bitterest of all was the thought that it was

his own sin which had brought this peril upon the inno-
cent." He had sent emissaries with presents to his
brother Esau, but they did not get any encouraging answer from him. They came back with the news that Esau
approached with four hundred armed men to meet his
brother Jacob, who, years ago, had robbed him of his
birthright and all the blessings that went with it.

"With earnest cries and tears he [Jacob] made his
prayer before God. Suddenly a strong hand was laid
upon him. He thought that an enemy was seeking his
life, and he endeavored to wrest himself from the grasp
of his assailant. . . . While he was thus battling for his
life, the sense of his guilt pressed upon his soul; his sins
rose up before him, to shut him out from God. But in his
terrible extremity he remembered God's promises, and
his whole heart went out in entreaty for His mercy."

We have to skip many details. You remember the
story. The patriarch, after failing to win over the
stranger, discerned at dawn the man's real identity. "It
was Christ, 'the Angel of the covenant,' who had revealed Himself to Jacob. The patriarch was now disabled
and suffering the keenest pain, but he would not loosen
his hold. All penitent and broken, he clung to the Angel;
'he wept, and made supplication' (Hosea 12:4), pleading
for a blessing. He must have the assurance that his sin
was pardoned. Physical pain was not sufficient to divert
his mind from his object. His determination grew
stronger, his faith more earnest and persevering, until
the very last."

Jacob won the spiritual battle. "Through humilia-
tion, repentance, and self-surrender, this sinful, erring
mortal prevailed with the Majesty of heaven. He had
fastened his trembling grasp upon the promises of God,
and the heart of Infinite Love could not turn away the
sinner's plea."

While he prayed in agony, he gained victory and
received a new name. "Thy name shall be called no more

Jacob [deceiver], but Israel [victor, prince with God]: for as a prince hast thou power with God and with men, and hast prevailed" (Genesis 32:28).

Likewise, it is only as our soul agonizes in prayer that we experience a complete victory. Then the Lord changes our character and gives us a "new name" (Revelation 2:17).

Mental and Physical Anguish

"Jacob's experience during that night of wrestling and anguish represents the trial through which the people of God must pass just before Christ's second coming" (PP 201).

Mental struggle. Paralleling what happened with Jacob that dark night, God's people will experience intense spiritual struggle and mental anguish because of a temporary uncertainty about the forgiveness of their sins. But after fervent supplications and communion with God they will receive total peace and security.

Although they suffer severe persecution, their greatest anxiety will not result from any physical danger but the "fear that every sin has not been repented of, and that through some fault in themselves they will fail to realize the fulfillment of the Saviour's promise: I 'will keep thee from the hour of temptation, which shall come upon all the world' (Revelation 3:10). If they could have the assurance of pardon they would not shrink from torture or death" (GC 619).

"They afflict their souls before God, pointing to their past repentance of their many sins, and pleading the Saviour's promise: 'Let him take hold of My strength, that he may make peace with Me; and he shall make peace with Me' (Isaiah 27:5). Their faith does not fail because their prayers are not immediately answered. Though suffering the keenest anxiety, terror, and distress, they do not cease their intercessions. They lay hold of the strength of God as Jacob laid hold of the Angel; and the language of their souls is: 'I will not let Thee go, except Thou bless me' " (GC 619, 620).

But Jacob's attitude did not arise from presumption. It was real faith. He had repented from all his sins before. Otherwise at that crisis hour of struggle he could have lost his life.

The time of distress we will have to face requires a special faith, "a faith that can endure weariness, delay, and hunger—a faith that will not faint though severely tried" (GC 621). And it is not something we can improvise in an emergency. We must develop it every day. Thus we need to learn how to pray with intensity, pouring out our soul before God, pleading for forgiveness, cleansing, and liberation from sin and defects of character, so that when affliction comes we may exercise that faith naturally.

But thank God that after a period of apparently unheeded supplications the blessing of Heaven will come, and the experience will give birth to a great peace. But there will also come a time of severe persecution.

Terrible Persecution

As in the case of Paul, when he spoke of the Second Coming he presented himself as being alive among them, Mrs. White used the first person when she described the final persecution. "In the time of trouble," she said, "we all fled from the cities and villages, but were pursued by the wicked, who entered the houses of the saints with a sword. They raised the sword to kill us, but it broke, and fell as powerless as a straw. Then we all cried day and night for deliverance, and the cry came up before God" (EW 34).

"This small remnant, unable to defend themselves in the deadly conflict with the powers of earth that are marshaled by the dragon host, make God their defense.

The decree has been passed by the highest earthly authority that they shall worship the beast and receive his
mark under pain of persecution and death" (5T 213).

Although many of God's people will find refuge in
desolate and isolated places, in the mountains, in caves,
in the deserts, "many of all nations and of all classes,
high and low, rich and poor, black and white, will be cast
into the most unjust and cruel bondage. The beloved of
God pass weary days, bound in chains, shut in by prison
bars, sentenced to be slain, some apparently left to die of
starvation in dark and loathsome dungeons. No human
ear is open to hear their moans; no human hand is ready
to lend them help" (GC 626). The wrath of the great
enemy reaches its highest peak as he realizes that the
time left grows short (GC 623).

During the persecution, the redeemed will have scattered everywhere. "They are in different companies, and
in all parts of the earth; and they will be tried singly, not
in groups. Every one must stand the test for himself"
(4BC 1143). And they will constantly pray to God for
deliverance. "Day and night they cry unto God for deliverance. The wicked exult, and the jeering cry is heard:
'Where now is your faith? Why does not God deliver you
out of our hands if you are indeed His people?' . . . Like
Jacob, all are wrestling with God. Their countenances
express their internal struggle. Paleness sits upon every
face. Yet they cease not their earnest intercession" (GC
630).

In spite of the apparent circumstances, the angels of
God surround them, stand by their side in the dungeons
and prisons, protect them. At the appointed hour God
miraculously liberates them.

Purpose of the Time of Trouble

We may think that since God has completed the sealing at the end of the time of grace and since the redeemed

will not sin any more on account of an experience reached through a special work of the Holy Spirit, they will have no need for further character development. But that is not the case.

Although the saints will not sin, they will continue to grow. Jesus was sinless and perfect. Nevertheless, "though he were a Son, yet learned he obedience by the things which he suffered" (Hebrews 5:8). As one of its divinely appointed purposes, the time of trouble will produce similar transformations in God's people. "Terrible scenes are just before them, a time of trouble which will test the value of character. Those who have the truth abiding in them will then be developed" (1T 508).

The experience of Jacob during the night of his struggle with the Lord offers us a good illustration of the effect of the time of trouble on the afflicted Christians. "Jacob took firm hold of the angel in his distress, and would not let him go. As he made supplication with tears, the angel reminded him of his past wrongs, and endeavored to escape from Jacob, to test him and prove him. So will the righteous, in the day of their anguish, be tested, proved, and tried, to manifest their strength of faith, their perseverance and unshaken confidence in the power of God to deliver them" (3SG 132, 133). Their confidence in the Lord and their dependence on Him will grow much stronger, thus developing their character more.

"Those who exercise but little faith now, are in the greatest danger of falling under the power of satanic delusions and the decree to compel the conscience. And even if they endure the test they will be plunged into deeper distress and anguish in the time of trouble, because they have never made it a habit to trust in God. The lessons of faith which they have neglected they will be forced to learn under a terrible pressure of discouragement" (GC 622).

Moreover, some who have not learned during prosperous times to put their appetites under control and deny self will have to learn it under the most difficult circumstances. "The time of trouble is just before us; and then stern necessity will require the people of God to deny self, and to eat merely enough to sustain life; but God will prepare us for that time. In that fearful hour our necessity will be God's opportunity to impart His strengthening power, and to sustain His people" (1T 206).

But God has another great purpose in letting us pass through the last hour of anguish. Satan, the great rebel, accused God of arbitrarily requiring His created beings to comply with an unjust law impossible to fulfill. At that time, due to a special level of Christian experience that the redeemed have acquired before the end of the sealing process, they will be living testimonies for God before the whole universe. They will demonstrate the possibility of a life with no sin, a life of perfect obedience. It will not be just an isolated human being here and there who will be able to show the falsehood of Satan's accusation but the whole host of the redeemed. By a total surrender to God and by the power of His Spirit they will live a sinless life, testifying to God's justice and His perfect law.

Our Only Safety During the Trouble

We will not now deal with the matter of God's physical protection and the material security of His people. We will discuss that in the next chapter. Instead, we want to refer here briefly to spiritual safety and the success of the sealed and to their ability to go through persecution victoriously.

To those of His children who would live in that dreadful hour, Christ sends a clear message. At the first glance it may seem too negative, too frank, since it denounces mainly a self-deceived people. They have doctrinal knowledge. Heresy is not their problem. But from the spiritual and practical viewpoint, the people of Laodicea are sorely misguided and self-sufficient. And they do not know it.

In spite of the apparent hopeless attitude of self-righteousness, the message presents a wonderful hope. The Great Physician offers remedies capable of completely preparing a people to go triumphantly through the terrible time, to meet the Lord in peace, and to be ready for translation.

Open the door of your heart, Jesus pleads. Repent. Buy of Me the gold of faith and love, the white robe of an imparted character woven in the loom of heaven, and the eyesalve of the Holy Spirit. If you do that, you will stand among "them that . . .[have] gotten the victory over the beast, and over his image, and over his mark, and over the number of his name," among those who "stand on the sea of glass, having the harps of God" (Revelation 15:2).

But God's remedies are good only before the end of probation. The sole source from which we can obtain them is Christ, the Physician of heaven. And we may obtain them only through a close experience with Him through daily surrender, prayer, Bible study, and active witnessing.

Chapter 6

The Time of Trouble, Part 2

Some Seventh-day Adventists prefer not to think about the time of trouble or discuss the issues involved in it. First, because they believe it a negative subject that alarmist minds like to speculate on. Second, because it makes the believers seek God from fear and not from love. And third, because they think that we should not disturb people about something awful that lies in the future.

Referring to the first objection, we answer that it is not negative, since it has to do with our eternal salvation. It is a reality all of us, as children of God, will have to face soon if God does not call us to rest. We do not need to apologize for dealing with an experience that the church will one day have to cope with. God allows it to occur for the benefit of His children, and He reveals it to us beforehand. One would not think that to consider an imminent danger and prepare to face it warrants labeling it an alarmist's attitude. To the contrary, it is rather a matter of good and sound judgment to make the necessary provisions.

On the other hand, the matter of the time of trouble, far from being a negative issue, is a most positive one. As we learn all the facts God has revealed to us in His Word and in the writings of Ellen G. White, the many wonderful promises of Christ's companionship, the ministry of the holy angels, His divine protection, and at last our miraculous delivery, it greatly increases our faith and strongly encourages our confidence. Also as we study the Word, it should draw us to an experience of personal repentance, revival, and reformation.

Regarding the second objection, God is ready to receive us as we are, even though our motive may not be the best one. Then, in our daily contact with Him and under the influence of the Spirit, we will change to the right motive. God's mercy is so great that He willingly takes us back, even though we fear Him. He repeatedly accepted apostate Israel back, even when they turned to Him because of the punishment He permitted the nation to suffer, whether political submission, defeat in warfare, or other calamities.

The third objection—that it will still be some time before the hour of trial and trouble will come—is one of Satan's favorite weapons. The parable of the ten virgins suggests that at least half of the church may not be prepared for the coming of the Bridegroom. The foolish Christians would not have obtained the essential element needed for them to receive Him, the oil of the Spirit, which reveals itself in a deep experience with Christ and in a character ready for translation.

The Seven Last Plagues

Somebody has written that "these last plagues are manifestations of the wrath of Satan and his work of deceit and destruction." Nevertheless, time after time both the Bible and the writings of Mrs. White refer to these great calamities as judgments of God: "God's judgments will be visited upon those who are seeking to oppress and destroy His people. His long forbearance with the wicked emboldens men in transgression, but their punishment is nonetheless certain and terrible because it is long delayed" (GC 627).

Do the two statements conflict? Not at all. It is not God that deliberately sends destruction and arbitrarily creates plagues to punish humanity. What simply happens is that God no longer curbs satanic wrath; He allows human passion to take its course without restriction.

Now the four angels hold back the winds of strife and passion in obedience to a command from God. But when the time of trouble begins, when the investigative judgment ceases and Christ ends His intercessory work, the angels will not restrain the winds any more. It is Satan who destroys and takes pleasure in doing so. God permits him to do it only because humanity's hour of opportunity has passed and no more hope and possibility of repentance exists.

"The records of the past—the long procession of tumults, conflicts and revolutions, the 'battle of the warrior . . . with confused noise, and garments rolled in blood' (Isaiah 9:5)—what are these, in contrast with the terrors of that day when the restraining Spirit of God shall be wholly withdrawn from the wicked, no longer to hold in check the outburst of human passion and satanic wrath! The world will then behold, as never before, the results of Satan's rule" (GC 36, 37). Even now "the wrath of Satan increases as his time grows short, and his work of deceit and destruction will reach its culmination in the time of trouble" (GC 623).

During the time of trouble the whole universe will witness in a world full of turmoil and destruction the awful results of Satan's rulership. They will see the complete falsity of his accusation that the law of God is unjust and impossible to fulfill. In the most difficult circumstances, while surrounded by strife, persecution, and threat of death, all the redeemed will fulfill the law with the help of God. Keeping their character unpolluted, they vindicate God, His law, His character, and His wisdom.

Protection and Tender Care of God

Along with Biblical promises of God's protection
(such as Psalms 27:5; 33:19; 91; Isaiah 26:20, 21; 33:16;
41:17), we find a wide variety and multiplicity of assurances in the writings of Ellen White.

First of all, none of the seven plagues will affect the
children of God in the least. But in order to stand the test
and enjoy the protection of God they need a genuine
relationship with the Lord.

"A form of godliness will not save any. All must have
a deep and living experience. This alone will save them
in the time of trouble. Then their work will be tried of
what sort it is; and if it is gold, silver and precious
stones, they will be hid as in the secret of the Lord's
pavilion. But if their work is wood, hay, and stubble,
nothing can shield them from the fierceness of Jehovah's
wrath" (1T 125).

"I saw a covering that God was drawing over His
people to protect them in the time of trouble; and every
soul that was decided on the truth and was pure in heart
was to be covered with the covering of the Almighty"
(EW 43).

"Fearful tests and trials await the people of God. . . .
But in the midst of the time of trouble that is coming—a
time of trouble such as has not been since there was a
nation—God's chosen people will stand unmoved. Satan
and his angels cannot destroy them, for angels that excel
in strength will protect them" (2SM 55). The following
statement emphasizes the thought even more. "Satan
with all the hosts of evil cannot destroy the weakest of
God's saints" (PK 513). The author refers to the same
time in both quotations.

God has more than enough power to fulfill His direct
promise. He has said, "Come out of her [Babylon], my
people, that ye be not partakers of her sins, and that ye
receive not of her plagues" (Revelation 18:4). So they

clearly will be totally free from the plagues.

Two outstanding characteristics of the time of trouble will be persecution and famine. For both contingencies we have precious promises reiterated over and over again.

Deliverance From Persecution and Death

"Those who have mocked at the idea of the saints' going up will witness the care of God for His people and behold their glorious deliverance. As the saints left the cities and villages, they were pursued by the wicked, who sought to slay them. But the swords that were raised to kill God's people broke and fell as powerless as a straw. Angels of God shielded the saints. As they cried day and night for deliverance, their cry came up before the Lord" (EW 284, 285).

We repeat here that after the close of probation, "God would not suffer the wicked to destroy those who were expecting translation and who would not bow to the decree of the beast or receive his mark" (EW 284). The time of trouble will have no martyrs.

Mrs. White repeats God's pledge of protection time after time. "God's love for His children during the period of their severest trial is as strong and tender as in the days of their sunniest prosperity" (GC 621).

"The heavenly sentinels, faithful to their trust, continue their watch. Though a general decree has fixed the time when commandment keepers may be put to death, their enemies will in some cases anticipate the decree, and before the time specified, will endeavor to take their lives. But none can pass the mighty guardians stationed about every faithful soul. Some are assailed in their flight from the cities and villages; but the swords raised against them break and fall powerless as a straw. Others are defended by angels in the form of men of war" (GC 631).

Not all will be able to flee. Many find themselves in prison. But even so, the angels accompany them to encourage and to protect. "Though enemies may thrust them [the children of God during the time of trouble] into prison, yet dungeon walls cannot cut off the communication between their souls and Christ. One who sees their every weakness, who is acquainted with every trial, is above all earthly powers; and angels will come to them in lonely cells, bringing light and peace from heaven. The prison will be as a palace; for the rich in faith dwell there, and the gloomy walls will be lighted up with heavenly light as when Paul and Silas prayed and sang praises at midnight in the Philippian dungeon" (GC 627).

Deliverance From Famine

One of the most terrible effects of the plagues will be drought and famine. But from both hazards God protects His people. Scripture promises that His child "shall dwell on high: his place of defence shall be the munitions of rocks: bread shall be given him; his waters shall be sure" (Isaiah 33:16).

Mrs. White applied the passage to the condition of God's people during the time of trouble. Persecuted, they flee to the mountains where "the munitions of rocks" shall be their defense, and where they have assurance of bread and water (GC 626).

"The people of God will not be free from suffering; but while persecuted and distressed, while they endure privation and suffer from want of food they will not be left to perish. . . . While the wicked are dying from hunger and pestilence, angels will shield the righteous and supply their wants. To him that 'walketh righteously' is the promise: 'Bread shall be given him; his waters shall be sure.' 'When the poor and needy seek water, and there is none, and their tongue faileth for

thirst, I the Lord will hear them, I the God of Israel will
not forsake them.' Isaiah 33:15, 16; 41:17" (GC 629).

"I saw that our bread and water will be sure at that
time, and that we shall not lack or suffer hunger; for God
is able to spread a table for us in the wilderness. If
necessary He would send ravens to feed us, as He did to
feed Elijah, or rain manna from heaven, as He did for the
Israelites" (EW 56).

No More Mediator; No More Probation

Although it may be difficult for us to understand how
the saints will reach a sinless state at the close of probation, because they will have no more Mediator and hence
no more opportunity of repenting, we can trust in the
Lord and in His promises and take God at His word. But
we need to fulfill our part. And we must do it now while
the sealing is still in process.

The Lord has given His last generation more light,
more knowledge, more spiritual incentives, than any
prior generation of history. God never requires an im-
possibility. He provides the power to meet His com-
mands if we will make complete surrender and a total
and continued commitment to Him.

The parable of the ten virgins tells of a great danger: a
substantial part of the church may not take advantage of
all the opportunities available today, postponing the
dedication of time and efforts needed to have a real
relationship with the Lord.

In the back of the mind of many a Seventh-day Adventist lurks the unexpressed thought that we still have
some time before we must seriously prepare for the hour
when heaven issues the decree which ends the time of
salvation. We may have some favorite project in hand,
some study program, some special assignment, that
crowds out the time we must spend with God. Thus we
keep on procrastinating something that should have first

priority. Jesus urges us to abandon the circle of the
foolish virgins and to begin securing the oil of the Spirit
that gives a character ready for translation.

Near But Unexpected

In 1904 Ellen White wrote, "Soon grievous troubles
will arise among the nations—trouble that will not cease
until Jesus comes. As never before we need to press
together, serving Him who has prepared His throne in
the heavens, and whose kingdom ruleth over all. . . . The
judgments of God are in the land. The wars and rumors
of wars, the destruction by fire and flood, say clearly that
the time of trouble, which is to increase until the end, is
very near at hand. "We have no time to lose. The world is
stirred with the spirit of war. The prophecies of the
eleventh of Daniel have almost reached their final fulfillment" (WM 136).

The Lord could have come already. But the delay
occurred for two reasons. First, the church was not prepared. The people at large did not possess the character
of Christ. Second, the church did not finish her task of
spreading God's last message of mercy. The second
cause results from the first. God has hundreds of
thousands of children in all communities. Sincere
people, they would respond at once should the Spirit of
God move on them with the power described in Revelation 18. But our church is not prepared to receive them,
and God in His mercy delays the hour, giving us time.

The day will arrive, though, when the Bridegroom, in
spite of the delay, will come. May He not find any one of
us in the condition of the foolish girls in the parable.

Only the Sealed Will Enter

In the parable of the marriage feast (Matthew 22:1-14)
the king said to his servants, "The wedding is ready, but

they which were bidden were not worthy. Go ye therefore into the highways, and as many as ye shall find, bid to the marriage.'' When the servants had gathered together as many as they could, the king inspected them.

As he looked over the guests "he saw there a man which had not on a wedding garment: and he saith unto him, Friend, how camest thou in hither not having a wedding garment? And he was speechless. Then said the king to the servants, Bind him hand and foot, and take him away, and cast him into outer darkness; there shall be weeping and gnashing of teeth. For many are called, but few are chosen.''

Everyone, both good and bad, received an invitation to the feast, with only one condition: that he would put on a special garment the king provided for the occasion. As we know, that special suit represents the robe of the righteousness of Christ, offered by the Heavenly King to everyone.

"By the wedding garment in the parable is represented the pure, spotless character which Christ's true followers will possess. To the church it is given 'that she should be arrayed in fine linen, clean and white,' 'not having spot, or wrinkle, or any such thing' (Revelation 19:8). The fine linen, says the Scripture, 'is the righteousness of saints' (Ephesians 5:27). It is the righteousness of Christ, His own unblemished character, that through faith is imparted to all who receive Him as their personal Saviour'' (COL 310).

"This robe, woven in the loom of heaven, has in it not one thread of human devising. Christ in His humanity wrought out a perfected character, and this character He offers to impart to us'' (COL, 311).

Only those dressed with the heavenly robe that the king gave could attend the feast. And only those who possess that character will inherit salvation. At the close of probation only those sealed by the living God will make it through the great hour of crisis and meet the

Lord in peace. "None but the hundred and forty-four thousand [the sealed] can learn that song; for it is the song of their experience. . . . They have passed through the time of trouble such as never was since there was a nation; they have endured the anguish of the time of Jacob's trouble" (GC 649).

Should it discourage us? Not at all. For we can obtain the character we need. The King is ready to give it to us—is actually eager for us to acquire it. It is not something reserved to a few that have more possibilities than the rest of us because of a privileged inheritance or a special environment or education. "By His perfect obedience He has made it possible for every human being to obey God's commandments." The condition is that "when we submit ourselves to Christ, the heart is united with His heart, the will is merged in His will, the mind becomes one with His mind, the thoughts are brought into captivity to Him; we live His life. This is what it means to be clothed with the garment of His righteousness" (COL 312).

Key to Success

This is the kind of preparation we need. A faith that translates itself into a continual surrender of the will, an opening up to the power of God to change life and character.

We receive imputed righteousness through an experience of repentance and confession of sin and forgiveness of those sins. Our repentance is so real that it produces the fruits of righteousness. The imputed righteousness of Christ naturally leads us to acquire His imparted character. Contemplating His character reproduces the image of Christ in our lives. It means a transformation of heart not reserved to just a few but to every born-again Christian who pays the price. What is that price? Repentance. **Surrender. Time with God. Victory.**

Chapter 7

Spiritualism and the Occult

Ours is an age of an extraordinary upsurge of spiritualism and the occult. People everywhere, in all walks of life, desperately search for something new to solve their spiritual problems, to heal their sick minds and bodies.

Spiritualism and all related activities present themselves as healing balms. When associated with the claim that it is the sure means of crossing the frontier of death and communicating with deceased loved ones, it exerts an almost irresistible attraction to everybody not acquainted with the Word of God.

Undeniable evidence of supernatural phenomena that one cannot explain by the action of natural laws greatly increases the impact of spiritualistic and occult forces.

It will become even more forceful in the future. Many refuse to accept the concept of the supernatural, but they will face phenomena that they cannot deny by the senses or by the tests of science. Forced to admit the reality and the authenticity of such supernormal manifestations, they will also adopt the idea that their claim has come from God and the spirits of the dead. Then the deception will be global in its extension and total in its human appeal. With the exception of the Christians well grounded through study of the Bible and through a real experience with the Lord, everyone will fall prey to such phenomena. Studying, praying Christians are the only ones who will be able to withstand the temptation of the devil, resisting even the apparent evidence of the senses, because they have deeply rooted themselves in the Word of God and let the Spirit guide them.

Since it will be one of the favorite ways in which the enemy will work in the last days, and since we do not know under what new and deceiving disguises Satan will present himself, a real danger exists even for Seventh-day Adventists. "Satan himself" will be "transformed into an angel of light" (2 Corinthians 11:14). Christ said, "There shall rise false Christs, and false prophets, and shall shew great signs and wonders; insomuch that, if it were possible, they shall deceive the very elect. Behold, I have told you before" (Matthew 24:24, 25).

Genesis and Development of Spiritualistic Phenomena

Spiritualism had its inception right in Eden. Soon after Creation Satan came to tempt Adam and Eve and cause them to break God's law and lose their happiness. But he did not present himself as an angel, lest Eve would suspect that he was the terrible enemy about which the angels had warned her and Adam. The angels had explained his revolution in heaven, his war against God, and his consequent expulsion.

Instead, Satan disguised himself as a speaking animal. He used the serpent, one of Eden's most attractive creatures. Mrs. White tells us that "the serpent was then one of the wisest and most beautiful creatures on the earth. It had wings, and while flying through the air presented an appearance of dazzling brightness, having the color and brilliancy of burnished gold. Resting in the rich-laden branches of the forbidden tree and regaling itself with the delicious fruit, it was an object to arrest the attention and delight of the beholder" (PP 53).

Eve had no thought at all that the dazzling creature could be the deceiver. With great curiosity, mingled with amazement at the thought of a speaking serpent, she began an apparently harmless dialogue with Satan that ended with her accepting his lie instead of the explicit word of God.

Thus Eden was the setting for the first spiritistic séance, and the serpent the first medium. The only difference was that the serpent did not have the power to refuse to serve as Satan's instrument. Present-day mediums do, but they willingly offer themselves to the great deceiver, although most of the time without knowing into which hands they put themselves.

From that tragic moment at the dawn of earth's history to the present day the devil and his angels have actively produced all types of spiritualistic phenomena. And from that first lie—"Ye shall not surely die"—arose all pagan and false Christian religions. Moreover, that first lie, along with the false rest day, will link together the last confederacy of evil powers.

Both in the Old and in the New testaments we have plenty of demonstrations of spiritualistic activities, including consultations with the "spirits" of the dead, demon possession, divination, witchcraft, and so forth (Deuteronomy 18:10, 11; 1 Samuel 28; 2 Kings 1:1-4; Luke 8:26-39; Acts 8:9; 13:8; 16:16-18). All of them have the same origin—the devil, the first liar and the father of every lie (John 8:44). God had good reasons to prohibit in the most definite terms all such activities and any relationship at all with any form of spiritualistic phenomena (Deuteronomy 18:10-12; Leviticus 20:27, 6).

Modern Manifestations

Although the modern phase of spiritualism began in Hydesville, New York, in 1848 with the rappings in the house of the Fox family, the methods and the names used by the archdeceiver have evolved tremendously from that time. They have so many different facets, some of them so attractive, that unless we constantly remain on our guard, even we members of the remnant church could easily fall into Satan's snares.

We live today in a decade of extraordinary thirst for the supernatural. People are starving for something different. What the traditional religions offer them does not satisfy because it does not answer life's great problems. Thus all kinds of satanic activities are popular.

Witchcraft, sorcery, and magic still attract the less-educated people, both in pagan and in Christian countries. Spiritualists' schools and societies meeting under a religious guise in halls continue to have their spell on a great segment of the population of many countries. In their meetings they invoke God's name and sing hymns. Some of the societies are so aristocratic as to attract the wealthy and the educated. Others enroll the scientifically minded.

After the author had finished publishing a series of articles in the Spanish language missionary magazine *Vida Feliz* some years ago, he received a letter inviting him to the luxurious hall of the most prominent and aristocratic spiritualistic society of Argentina. The letter said, in part, "We have been reading your interesting articles, and we invite you to a public meeting in our hall to give us a lecture and answer some questions."

The temptation to accept was great. But after reading again and considering the guidelines Ellen White has given us, we decided to decline. In the most gracious way possible we explained that if we went to their hall, we probably would be obligated to make some statements directly in opposition to the beliefs of spiritualism, and that would be painful to us. Instead, we organized a series of public meetings in our main church downtown, and invited the ones interested to come and study at our place.

The prohibition of the Lord against having any relationship with spiritualism comprises not only attending the séances but also reading or simply possessing books that contain spiritualistic formulas or prayers or that explain the techniques used by the occult. In many areas of the world we would have to avoid even allowing a man or woman that Satan is using to live on our premises.

Some years ago a strange experience took place in Argentina. One day unusual things began to happen in the home of one of the elders of a certain church. At night rocks would fall on the roof and the walls and doors of the house. Despite fervent prayers it happened night after night. Then the troubles began inside. Different objects would rise from the table or cabinets and plummet to the ground for no apparent reason. One day as the mother mixed dough for bread, suddenly it rose from the table by itself and dropped to the floor.

Several days later the family discovered that a girl living in that house and helping in the domestic chores was demon possessed. They decided to send her away, and the poltergeist phenomena ceased.

The prohibition also refers to engaging in discussion or debates with spiritualistic leaders. "Men who bring in these damnable heresies [spiritualistic teachings] will dare those who teach the word of God to enter into controversy with them. . . . Some of our ministers have not had the moral courage to say no to these men: God has warned us in His word in regard to you. He has given us a faithful description of your character and of the heresies which you hold. Some of our ministers, rather than give this class any occasion to triumph or to charge them with cowardice, have met them in open discussion. But in discussing with spiritualists they do not meet man merely, but Satan and his angels. They place themselves in communication with the powers of darkness and encourage evil angels about them" (3T 485).

Some definite occasions may arise in which we find it absolutely necessary to debate with Spiritualists. In those cases, we should accept the challenge only after making sure that we have taken several precautions.

1. The people engaged in the debate should have a real relationship with God. They should understand they are dealing with Satan and his angels. They should recognize their human weakness for the task and wholly depend upon God for direction.

2. Never should one person alone meet the Spiritualists, but several, and while one speaks the rest should pray for the presence of the Spirit of God. (Read the interesting case related in *Testimonies*, Vol. 1, pages 426-429.)

Some churches will turn the Sunday morning service over to faith healers who are openly Spiritualists. The Church of Satan is obviously satanic. And those who dabble in astrology and who play with the Ouija board open themselves up to the influence of the enemy.

Parapsychology claims to be a scientific discipline studying extrasensory perceptions and other paranormal phenomena, like telekinesis (moving of objects or persons from one place to another by unknown and unseen powers), clairvoyance (the faculty of discerning objects not present to the senses), and telepathy (transmission of thought). But parapsychology—although regarding itself as a purely scientific activity without any relationship to spiritualism, devoting itself to examining a series of "paranormal" phenomena to discover their yet unknown laws—actually deals with things that may have satanic origin.

Spiritualism often involves hypnotism. The mediumistic trance parallels what happens in the deep state of hypnosis, where another personality takes control of the human mind and body.

In the deep hypnosis the subject falls under the control of the hypnotizer, responding to his voice and suggestions. The conscious mind does not function any more. Mrs. White has made several statements linking hypnotism and Satan (MH 242, 243; EW 21). In one place she wrote, "His agents [those of the prince of darkness] still claim to cure disease. [The author is speaking about the hypnotism of her day, then called magnetism.] They attribute their power to electricity, magnetism, or the so-called sympathetic remedies. In truth, they are but channels for *Satan's electric currents*. By this means he casts his spell over the bodies and souls of men" (2TT 52).

The Source of These Phenomena

No science, no psychology, no proven theory, can explain all the supernormal phenomena that happen in spiritualistic activities. The Word of God describes the intelligent unseen forces that are at work as the "rulers of the darkness," the "spiritual wickedness in high places" (Ephesians 6:12).

God's people face a dilemma in convincing the nonbeliever about Satan's active role. Only by the authority of God's revelation can we establish the satanic origin of spiritualism, since it is beyond human research.

Evil spirits claim to be the spirits of the dead, and unless a person firmly believes in the inspiration of the Bible, he faces great pressure to accept their statements. The picture is further complicated because almost all the Christian churches, as well as pagan religions, accept the doctrine of immortality of the soul and its survival after death.

Appeal of Spiritualism on Human Minds

The human mind is man's citadel. In it resides the God-given power of choice and the sense of responsibil-

ity. It is the seat of our personality, regulating our acts,
our ideas, our feelings and emotions. Whether we build
a character that will stand the test of time or one that will
resist God's offer of salvation depends upon the right use
of the mind and the faculties that make us similar to God:
the will, the power to make decisions. That is why Satan
constantly attempts to subdue our minds and our wills,
whether by deception, force, or appeal to our physical
senses and their momentary satisfaction.

But God also does not ignore us. His love follows us,
His Spirit pleads with us, always encouraging us to use
our willpower to surrender voluntarily to Him. He never
forces us. Christianity is eminently a religion of freedom, and when imposed upon somebody, it loses its
meaning.

Are Spiritualism and Related Activities Compatible With Christianity?

As a teenager I belonged to the Methodist Church.
One day I discovered, to my surprise, that a famous
Methodist pastor I knew was involved in spiritualistic
activities. Instinctively I felt amazement, because somehow I had the idea that spiritualism was against Christian principles. Then I reasoned, Why not? The spirits of
the dead are somewhere. What is wrong with trying to
contact them? And if spiritualism is the method to do it,
we should naturally welcome it. But when I was nineteen
years old, totally unsatisfied and with many questions
that I still had not found answers for, I began studying
the Bible for myself. What in former years seemed
natural soon became unbiblical and incompatible with
Christianity.

Thousands upon thousands of Protestant ministers
and leaders not only accept and practice spiritualism as a
complement to their religion, but they also belong to and
lead spiritualistic societies, sometimes disguised under

more attractive names. Even we can spot the mediums among them.

We as Seventh-day Adventists have the correct knowledge about the true state of the dead, and we know that the main teachings of spiritualism and its whole philosophy openly contradict what God has revealed in the Bible. An October 27, 1977, editorial in the *Review and Herald* stated that "because God knew the machinations that Satan would use to deceive the elect, in kindness and love for our spiritual safety He made this seemingly peripheral doctrine one of the landmarks of the Seventh-day Adventist Church. The importance of this subject may not be fully apparent now, but the time is not far distant when, in the face of empirical evidence to the contrary, our adherence to Scripture will be tested."

Spiritualism violates Biblical teaching not only in the deception it teaches regarding the state of the dead and the identity of the evil spirits but also in its conception of the plan of redemption. According to it, life eternal is not a gift that we receive freely from God only by the acceptance of Jesus Christ as our personal Saviour. To the contrary, it is something that man acquires by his own means and efforts as he goes through different stages of reincarnation. Life is not the only opportunity we have to prepare a character fit for heaven, but one of many existences that the human being may have, they maintain.

When we were young students at the university, a Seventh-day Adventist schoolmate received an invitation to present a lecture about the Bible in a Spiritualists' hall. Several of his fellow students, members of the Adventist Church, went with him to pray while he spoke. God blessed him in spite of the heavy atmosphere that one could detect in that meeting. On our way outside the hall, as we waited for the elevator, an impressive-looking man came up to us. He complimented the speaker, then added, "But remember, we Spiritualists are much farther ahead than the Bible. We have surpassed it in many respects and are more advanced in our knowledge." Naturally, the Spiritualists do not consider the Bible as the genuine revelation of God, but as a book that they can change and reinterpret according to new insights obtained through the spirits.

We as Christians have three tests to discover the soundness of any doctrine in the world: (1) if it agrees with the teachings of the law and the testimonies (the Word of God); (2) by the fruits, that is, the results, of that particular doctrine; (3) if it accepts Jesus as the Son of God, the Saviour of humanity. And the third point means recognition of the sinful human condition and the individual's need for repentance, confession, surrender to God, and willingness to do His will and fulfill His commandments.

In all three proofs spiritualism fails and appears as the deceptive creation of God's great enemy.

The Only Source of True Knowledge, Healing, and Happiness

One great reason for the growing popularity of spiritualism and the occult is that human beings, sick and tired of sin, are looking for some solution for their spiritual problems. Call it charismatic movement, astrology, or psychic research, everybody has an inner craving for peace and happiness. Satan, as a great psychologist, offers to satisfy it.

But humanity has had already sixty centuries of experience to discover that the claims of the fallen archangel are a lie. Millions of people, accepting the tempting answer that Satan presents to their problems, have found only desperation, misery, and eternal death.

There exists only one source of true knowledge, of physical and spiritual health, and of real happiness:

Jesus. By the well of Samaria He told the woman, "Whosoever drinketh of this water [all merely human means and material things] shall thirst again: but whosoever drinketh of the water that I shall give him shall never thrist; but the water that I shall give him shall be in him a well of water springing up into everlasting life" (John 4:13, 14).

The promises of spiritualism are only tinsel. Satan uses them to trap people. True, in the last moments before Christ's return he will sometimes remove causes of physical sickness that he himself introduced, thus appearing to perform great miracles of healing. But he does it solely to snare the person and finally destroy him. Spiritualism may even voice some Christian truths in order to mix with them as much error as possible. No permanent good can result when a person resorts to any method or instrument of Satan.

Some people resort to psychiatry. If practiced by a well-informed doctor and a good Christian professional, it can do much good, when used as a means to take the individual to Christ. The majority of human psychic illnesses have sin as their main cause. But in itself, completely devoid of Christ, psychiatry has no real answer to human problems.

The deep longing of the human heart finds an absolute remedy in the words and in the person of the One that said, "Peace I leave with you, my peace I give unto you: not as the world giveth, give I unto you. Let not your heart be troubled, neither let it be afraid" (John 14:27).

Chapter 8

Spiritualism
and Bible Prophecy

The fact that so many prophecies regarding last-day events deal with spiritualism and related activities indicates that it will play a major role in the historic and religious developments of the final hours of human history.

Satan and his host of wicked angels retain much of the power and wisdom they had before they sinned, and they apply all of it to deception and destruction. In addition, Satan has by now a lot of experience in dealing with human beings. Moreover, he reserves his great master deception for the last moment, when he will try to imitate the second coming of Christ.

God has given us the prophecies of the Bible for four main reasons. The first one is to provide every sincere student with an undeniable foundation of Scriptural divine inspiration. Second, they give us absolute confidence in the fact that amid the apparent confusion of human activity God has His omnipotent hand on the helm of history and that He leads in the affairs of nations. In the final end His sovereignty will prevail. His plan of restoration will succeed. Jesus will come, sin and suffering will end, and He will establish His eternal kingdom of glory and happiness. Third, they give His faithful children a clear indication in which development stage of God's plans they are living. Particularly it applies to our own generation. "When these things begin to come to pass, then look up, and lift up your heads; for your redemption draweth nigh" (Luke 21:28).

The fourth reason is not of any less importance: to prevent deception and unmask falsehood. In His wisdom and providence, God foresaw that in the last days of sin's history the forces of evil would resort to any possible devices to ensnare the unwary, and even to confuse, if at all possible, God's people themselves.

So in His Sacred Word He described those forces, predicted their movements and operation, and opened before us their devices and real intention, thus warning us about events so that we would not mistakenly accept error. Jesus said, "If any man will do his will, he shall know of the doctrine, whether it be of God" (John 7:17).

Deceitful Miracles and Satanic Delusions

Revelation 16:13, 14 portrays the three powers that will unite their efforts to delude. The dragon, which in the first place is Satan (Revelation 12:9), in chapter 13 works through the Roman Empire, but here in chapter 16 it represents spiritualism. The beast is the Christian Roman power, and the false prophet is the United States allied with apostate Protestantism.

In *The Great Controversy*, page 588, we find a comment on Revelation 16:13, 14 which presents an equivalent for each of the three. But in volume 5 of *Testimonies* we also find a direct reference to the unholy alliance: "When Protestantism [united with the State and using its civil power] shall stretch her hand across the gulf to grasp the hand of the Roman power [papacy], when she shall reach over the abyss to clasp hands with spiritualism, when, under the influence of this threefold union, our country shall repudiate every principle of its Constitution as a Protestant and republican government, and shall make provision for the propagation of papal falsehoods and delusions, then we may know that the time has come for the marvelous working of Satan and that the end is near."

Mrs. White goes on to say, "As the approach of the Roman armies was a sign to the disciples of the impending destruction of Jerusalem, so may this apostasy be a sign to us that the limit of God's forbearance is reached, that the measure of our nation's iniquity is full, and that the angel of mercy is about to take her flight, never to return. The people of God will then be plunged into those scenes of affliction and distress which prophets have described as the time of Jacob's trouble" (5T 451).

The passages first indicate the extraordinary growth of spiritualism and its increasing involvement with Protestantism on the one hand and with Romanism on the other. We can see a great bond developing between the three groups through healing activities in great Protestant assemblies and in evangelical worship hours. Also, Roman Catholic healing evidently results from the same power.

Glossolalia, both in the traditional Pentecostal churches and today in widespread Protestant and Catholic congregations, offers another sign of union. Probably it will succeed where up to now ecumenism has failed.

As we mentioned before, the two great errors that separate the people of God from the rest of Protestantism—the belief in the conscious state of the dead and in the false sabbath, the one linking the churches with spiritualism and the other giving a common bond between Protestantism and Romanism—constitute two more powerful factors for such an alliance.

But we need to examine still another aspect of Revelation 16:13, 14. Out of the mouth of every one of the three powers emerge unclean spirits. Describing them, the prophet says that "they are the spirits of devils, working

miracles." In other words, spiritualism will be the outstanding element, so much so that it will be present
through the evil spirits in both Protestantism and
Romanism. We see how today spiritualism has saturated
both the Protestant and the Roman Catholic churches.

At the same time, the lines of demarcation of the
different traditional evangelical churches are slowly van-
ishing. Many churches have toned down or abandoned
features of doctrine that used to be basic to them, so that
they may not act as obstacles to the union sought for by
ecumenism.

Even the Roman Catholic Church, through the
policies adopted by Vatican Council II, has given the
impression of making important changes in order to
make itself more acceptable to the "separated brethren."
When one analyzes all of them, though, it is impossible
to substantiate any real alteration in the dogma or fundamental policies. But it has attracted the attention of the
evangelical faiths.

"Romanism is now regarded by Protestants with far
greater favor than in former years. [This is much more
evident now after Vatican II.] . . . The opinion is gaining
ground that, after all, we do not differ so widely upon
vital points as has been supposed, and that a little con-
cession on our part will bring us into a better understanding with Rome" (GC 563).

The real fact is, nevertheless, that "the papal church
will never relinquish her claim to infallibility" (GC 564).
"Romanism as a system is no more in harmony with the
gospel of Christ now than at any former period in her
history. The Protestant churches are in great darkness, or
they would discern the signs of the times" (GC 565).
"The Roman Church now presents a fair front to the
world, covering with apologies her record of horrible
cruelties . . . but she is unchanged" (GC 571). "Let it be
remembered, it is the boast of Rome that she never
changes" (GC 581).

The patterning of the Protestant churches after the Catholic is a process more advanced now than many suppose. And to complete the picture, spiritualism is infiltrating both religious sectors more and more.

The spirits of demons coming out of the mouth of the three powers will be in such good terms with human governments, whom they deceive and convince with miracles, that they lead them to join their cause, rallying them to the great battle of Armageddon. Armageddon is the great last effort of the wicked religiopolitical forces, commanded by Satan, to persecute and destroy God's people. But we will see that God will intervene to deliver His people and destroy evil (Revelation 19).

Paul, in 2 Thessalonians 2:8-10, refers to the "working of Satan," where he will attempt to capture humanity "with all power and signs and lying wonders, and with all deceivableness." The climax of process of world delusion appears in the prophecy of Revelation 13:13, 14, where the religiopolitical power made up by the state and apostate Protestantism, "doeth great wonders." It operates through spiritualism, the third ally, "so that he maketh fire come down from heaven on the earth in the sight of men, and deceiveth them that dwell on the earth by the means of those miracles which he had power to do in the sight of the beast."

The Master Attempt of Satan

We have not yet seen some of those great wonders, including that of fire coming down from heaven, unless it could refer in part to the modern UFOs. The year 1947 first saw discussion of the strange celestial phenomena in the news. Since then newspapers have reported the disconcerting sightings of unusual objects flying in the sky, sometimes approaching individuals or even groups of people. It has happened even in the most distant places of the world. Books, magazine articles, TV, and movies keep the subject in the spotlight.

Astronomers, pilots, military men, astronauts, and highly educated people have seen them to such extent that few now dismiss such reports as only hallucinations.

Up to now nobody has been able to give a real or satisfactory explanation of some of the sightings. Only if we see them in the perspective of Bible prophecy do they fall into place. They could well form part of Satan's strategy for the last days, in order little by little to gain the confidence of humanity and condition the world for the great master attempt that he will make to imitate the second coming of Jesus. We have been told that "as the crowning act in the great drama of deception, Satan himself will personate Christ" in His second coming (GC 624; see also 5BC 1106).

Yes, in fulfillment of Bible prophecies, "fearful sights of a supernatural character will soon be revealed in the heavens, in token of the power of miracle-working demons" (GC 624).

A Defense Against Deception

Eternal truth has just one source: "Thy word is truth" (John 17:17). In spiritual matters no other method can give us assurance about what is falsehood and what is truth. No empirical or rationalistic method can lead us to discover the truth. Only revelation, the inspired and eternal Word of God, can prevent deception.

"To the law and to the testimony: if they speak not according to this word, it is because there is no light in them" (Isaiah 8:20). The Word of God (the law and the testimony), is the only infallible touchstone to test any doctrine, any activity, any phenomenon, in order to find out its validity and its source, whether it comes from God or Satan.

Do we devote enough time to study the Scriptures?

Once Seventh-day Adventists had the reputation as people of the Book. Our pioneers, our Founding Fathers, used to devote whole days and nights to searching the Scriptures, praying with fervor for the leadership of the Holy Spirit, and according to the promise, that Spirit led them. They discovered one truth after another.

Unfortunately it is not that way anymore. Many church members devote little time to study for themselves but rely on the efforts of others. Sometimes they have only a vague idea of the teachings of the Bible. Such an imperfect and superficial knowledge cannot give them the assurance Paul had when he wrote, "I know whom I have believed, and am persuaded that he is able to keep that which I have committed unto him against that day" (2 Timothy 1:12). Paul also added, "The foundation of God standeth sure" (2 Timothy 2:19). To have that kind of assurance despite trials and hardship, even in the face of death as was his case, we need more than an accidental reading of the Bible once in a while. We need the accurate and thorough knowledge of it that results from a daily systematic study. In order to be physically strong and fit we need to eat every day and not depend on the meals that other people take. Likewise, we need to feed our spirit daily with the bread of life.

Probably the following condemnation would apply to many of us who do not study enough: "When for the time ye ought to be teachers, ye have need that one teach you again which be the first principles of the oracles of God; and are become such as have need of milk, and not of strong meat" (Hebrews 5:12). The period in which we live demands that we be teachers and not students learning the first elements of truth.

The Only Safeguard Against Spiritualism

But a mere intellectual, theoretical, or theological knowledge of the doctrines and prophecies, no matter how thorough it is, will not protect us from Satan. The fallen angel tries an infinite number of approaches and techniques. Spiritualistic teaching is one. But he does not rely only on it. He uses other avenues and tries to tempt every child of God in the precise aspect in which he is weak. "Satan studies every indication of the frailty of human nature, he marks the sins which each individual is inclined to commit, and then he takes care that opportunities shall not be wanting to gratify the tendency to evil" (GC 555). So, in order to become victorious over every attack of the enemy, we need to find the way of guarding ourselves in those particular points.

But we possess no power at all in us to stand firm against a foe that is much more powerful and astute than we are. Our only security resides in Jesus. "The power and malice of Satan and his host might justly alarm us," Mrs. White wrote, "were it not that we may find shelter and deliverance in the superior power of our Redeemer" (GC 517).

"Without me ye can do nothing" (John 15:5), Jesus said. On the other hand, "this is life eternal, that they might know thee the only true God, and Jesus Christ, whom thou hast sent" (John 17:3).

Now, in order to really know somebody we need to spend time with him. The only way of having a personal experience with Jesus is through the daily study and meditation of His Word (including the writings of Ellen White); spending enough time talking with Him through prayer, and looking into His beautiful and perfect character; responding to His love by a continual surrender of self; and witnessing about what He has done for us.

In the same way as we budget our expenses to meet our income, we need to portion our day to have time enough to sit at the feet of Jesus and to receive His grace.

Chapter 9

Glossolalia and
Charismatic Phenomena

The Eastern General Conference of Catholic Charismatic Renewal convened at the Convention Hall of Atlantic City in October, 1976, and for three consecutive days 28,000 Christians of different faiths (but mostly Roman Catholics) heard sermons and participated in the worship services. One of the main leaders of that movement, a Catholic priest, expressed the idea that the charismatic movement is one of the elements of a "process of reconciliation and unity" of the Christian church. Father Michael Scanlan said that God is "pouring out His Spirit on the Charismatic Renewal for Christian unity."

Four years earlier, in June, 1972, 20,000 had gathered for the charismatic renewal conference at the Catholic University of Notre Dame. The weekend meetings closed with a Sunday afternoon mass celebrated together by nearly five hundred priests, six bishops, and Cardinal Leo Joseph Suenens, head of the Catholic Church in Belgium. He had declared earlier his great faith in the charismatic movement, and said that he too had received "the baptism of the Holy Spirit" by speaking in tongues.

Two decades ago nobody would even dream that some of the most conservative churches would travel the road of the charismatic movement, much less that leaders of the Catholic Church would endorse it as a providential and orthodox method of achieving the unity of the churches aimed at by both the Vatican Council and the World Council of Churches.

Once again we see signs of unity among the three great powers—namely, the dragon (spiritism), the beast (papacy), and the false prophet (apostate Protestantism)—that Satan will use in his final thrust against God, His people, and His truth.

Today the hierarchs of the Roman church enthusiastically sponsor the charismatic movement, along with the Lutherans, the Episcopalians, and practically all the evangelical churches. The fact is, though, that a great similarity exists between the charismatic phenomena and some spiritistic activities. Taking advantage of the state of confusion that we see today in the Christian churches and the general spiritual thirst of people not satisfied with the coldness and ineffectiveness of their own faiths, Satan has emphasized a more emotional type of religion. Although it claims to be spiritual renewal, it is nothing less, in the last analysis, than a "Christianized form of spiritism," as editor Raymond F. Cottrell called it in his article in the *Review* of December 2, 1976.

The Authentic Gift of the Spirit

No one can deny the existence of an authentic gift of the Spirit called the gift of tongues (1 Corinthians 12:28). It is also evident that the first and main manifestation of the gift in the apostolic church happened on the day of Pentecost for the specific reason of declaring the good news about Jesus to people of about sixteen different nationalities, who were not familiar with the Aramaic language spoken in Jerusalem.

God decides what gift to bestow on the church and in what epoch, according to the particular need of that time and place. We may ask why we don't see many manifestations of the gift of tongues now. The answer is an easy one. In today's world, missionaries can learn how to

handle a new language in a comparatively easy and fast
way. They have good schools, dictionaries, grammars,
and opportunities to study. On the other hand, God saw
that in the kind of confused world we live in, the church
needed the clear voice of a modern prophet. He gave to
His church the gift of prophecy that has proved to be
such a tremendous blessing.

The gift of tongues had only three reported manifestations in the apostolic church. If it were something
absolutely indispensable in the experience of *every
Christian* to attest a real conversion—as Pentecostals
believe—the New Testament would constantly mention
the phenomenon. But that is not the case. If glossolalia
were a normative element in the life of every born-again
Christian, the silence of Luke regarding the three
thousand saved at Pentecost and the Samaritans in Acts 8
would be inexplicable.

The first and the main one of the three New Testament incidents took place at Pentecost, and as we saw,
the main objective was to reach pilgrims that spoke a
foreign language. In the other two—the encounter of
Peter with Cornelius (Acts 10:45, 46) and Paul's finding
the new converts in Ephesus (Acts 19:5, 6)—the objective
was twofold, namely, to convince the disciples of the
genuineness of the experience of the Gentiles and of
God's acceptance of them and to give the gifted the
ability to proclaim the gospel in other languages (AA
139, 281-283). But we should note that the two were
unique cases and their occurrence was a sign, not because the early Christians always expected such
phenomena, but precisely because they were unexpected and unusual.

1 Corinthians 14 and the Ecstatic Gift of Tongues

Some would see another type of Biblical speaking in
tongues in the fourteenth chapter of 1 Corinthians, espe-

cially verses 2 to 4. "He that speaketh in an unknown tongue speaketh not unto men, but unto God: for no man understandeth him; howbeit in the spirit he speaketh mysteries. But he that prophesieth speaketh unto men to edification, and exhortation, and comfort. He that speaketh in an unknown tongue edifieth himself; but he that prophesieth edifieth the church."

First of all, let's clarify that the word *unknown* is not in the original Greek. It is supplied by the translators.

This is apparently a different type of speaking in tongues: (a) The person who utters it does not speak to men but to God. (b) He speaks mysteries. Hence it may be an unknown tongue. (c) The purpose is to "edify" himself.

This is a controversial passage of Scripture, and our scholars interpret it in different ways. Some of them believe that it presents a different class of the gift of speaking in tongues. Some do not. But in order to give the charismatic movement the full benefit of the doubt, we will assume the first possibility.

In our denominational history we find at least one true case of such speaking in tongues. Ellen White did not accept it at first, but after God gave her a vision, she recognized it as an authentic one. (The full information appears in the *Review*, March 15, 1973, pp. 6, 7.) Such an example could provide a basis for accepting the interpretation of 1 Corinthians 14:2-4 as referring to a different kind of gift of tongues.

But we must not forget the many pages Mrs. White wrote about the dangers of glossolalia mixed with the physical display and emotionalism common in her day as in ours and the way she condemned and disapproved of it. "They have an unmeaning gibberish which they call the unknown tongue, which is unknown not only by man but by the Lord and all heaven. Such gifts are manufactured by men and women, aided by the great deceiver. Fanaticism, false excitement, false talking in

tongues, and noisy exercises have been considered gifts
which God has placed in the church" (1T 412-414).

The Particular Condition of the Church of Corinth

Let us remember the historic setting in which the
church acted. The Corinthian church was in a low
spiritual state, facing a series of tremendous problems. It
was a cosmopolitan church, established in a center of
paganism and vice. The temple of Venus or Aphrodite,
for example, contained one thousand prostitute priest-
esses that practiced licentious rites. The epistle mentions
sins and weaknesses that Paul wanted to correct.

Among the evils of the church of Corinth was a counterfeit or false gift of tongues which Paul attacks as contrary to Bible teachings. The people of Corinth consulted
sibyls, working for a specific pagan oracle. The woman
would go into a trance similar to the state in which the
spiritist mediums find themselves in their séances. The
sibyls would speak in a mysterious and unknown gibberish that the priest would interpret for the client. The
practice apparently infiltrated the church.

That church, which would glorify itself with the possession of the gift of tongues, according to what Paul
says in chapters 12 to 14 of 1 Corinthians, actually had a
counterfeit that he denounces as a falsehood. The apostle
devotes chapter 12 to present and classify the importance
of the gifts.

Considerations of Paul Regarding the Gift of Tongues

From a study of the three chapters the following
points stand out clearly:

1. It is the Spirit who bestows the gifts as He pleases,
so that the reception of a particular gift does not depend
on the will or the demand of the individual (1 Corinthians 12:11).

2. The diversity of gifts, regulated by the Holy Spirit, has as its main aim the spiritual health, the cooperative harmony, and the functional unity of the church as a body (verses 1-28).

3. Not all will have or can have the gift of tongues (verses 29, 30).

4. The gift of tongues is listed last, and it is wrong to make of it the main feature of the spiritual life (verses 8-10; 29-31).

The last verse of chapter 12 and the whole of chapter 13 show that there is "a more excellent way" than the gifts, namely, to have in the life the fruit of the Spirit, the fruit of love.

From chapter 14 we gather the following facts:

1. The gift of prophecy is superior to the gift of tongues (verses 1-5). The apostle makes a persistent effort to lessen the latter's importance. The church of Corinth apparently boasted about speaking in tongues.

2. If somebody is going to use a foreign or unknown language at the church, he has to interpret it or find somebody who can. In case he is not able to do so, he should keep quiet (verses 6-19, 27, 28).

3. Paul condemns the Corinthians and admonishes them to suspend the sad spectacle in which many speak, even simultaneously, in a strange language, without interpretation. Their behavior produces confusion, brings ridicule to the gospel, discredits the church, and distorts one of the main functions of the gift of tongues, that is, to preach the gospel and to present a sign of divine authenticity (verses 20-26).

4. Speaking in tongues in the church, besides requiring interpretation, should follow two other rules: (a) Not more than two or three persons should speak. (b) They should take turns and not speak simultaneously (verse 27).

5. Paul's last consideration is that "God is not the author of confusion, but of peace. . . . Let all things be done decently and in order" (verses 33-40).

Modern Glossolalia a Counterfeit

A counterfeit is not always easy to distinguish and never classifies itself under that name. Hence, the counsel of 1 John 4: 1 about trying the spirits whether they are of God is a most relevant one in a time of confusion and false prophets. Even if we take the position that 1 Corinthians 14 supports another kind of tongues-speaking than the one referred to in Acts, when analyzed correctly, it does not support either the traditional Pentecostalism or the modern charismatic movement. Not only that, it most forcefully and clearly condemns it.

A number of other Biblical points single out modern glossolalia as a counterfeit.

First of all, the movement dispenses with the law of God. According to Isaiah 8:20, to go against the law indicates a spurious origin. God does not contradict Himself. He shows us in His Word that "the law is holy, and the commandment holy, and just, and good" (Romans 7:12). Also Jesus said that His law cannot and will not be destroyed (Matthew 5:17-19) because it is the reflection of God's perfect character, and as God cannot change, neither can the law.

Isaiah 8:20 also states, "To the law and to the testimony." Anything or anybody that does not speak according to the testimony (the Word of God), the only measure of truth, we can know for sure has no light or any truth in it, but only darkness and deception.

Any movement not in full harmony with the Bible we must discard as false.

We see the charismatic renewal in nearly all churches, Catholic and Protestant alike, without regard to doctrinal interpretation. It is compatible with any Scriptural perspective. Morover, it induces people to rely completely on the claimed baptism of the Spirit shown by the gift of tongues. As a result it makes them conceited, because the reasoning behind it is that the people who speak in tongues have climbed to the highest possible degree of Christian experience, to a condition in which they do not need anything more, and from which they will never fall.

But any true gift of the Spirit will happen in the context of Biblical truth and in the setting of God's worldwide church. "God has set some in *the* church . . ." (1 Corinthians 12:28). Everything that happens in a church may not come of God, for all church positions are not according "to the law and to the testimony."

The second criterion we can use to discover truth and orthodoxy is its results (Matthew 7:16). Heaven does not bestow the gifts of the Spirit to any person without his first having the fruits of the Spirit. And after receiving what one claims to be the gift of the Spirit, those fruits should be even more evident in the life. But it does not happen this way. Many who supposedly receive the Spirit and speak in tongues have not shown a change of life-style.

On the other hand, the practical results of modern tongues-speaking indicate that the experience is detrimental to Christian life. Too often it leaves Christ out of the picture. The main thing is to speak in tongues, and when the believer achieves it, he thinks he does not need anything else. It makes people feel superior, brings division into the church, and plunges the individual into a false security.

The Enemy's Aim With the Charismatic Movement

People eagerly search for a real source of happiness and a solution for their many daily problems. They feel frustrated with their own churches, concluding that they are irrelevant for our modern age. Consequently they will grasp anything spectacular or exciting in hope of discovering how to dispose of their anxieties and sorrows, a real way of answering their uncertainties.

As a result, the occult and the psychic have become popular. This also explains why the emotional type of charismatic religion seems to satisfy people who do not have a real experience with God.

Satan has a specific aim behind modern glossolalia. He knows as well as we do that "before the final visitation of God's judgments upon the earth there will be among the people of the Lord such a revival of primitive godliness as has not been witnessed since apostolic times" (GC 464). This outpouring of God's power will enable the church of God to spread the gospel to every person living on our planet.

But it has always been Satan's plan to prevent revival and reform, and he seeks to do it through a false revival. "The enemy of souls desires to hinder this work [the real outpouring of the Spirit]; and before the time for such a movement shall come, he will endeavor to prevent it by introducing a counterfeit. In those churches which he can bring under his deceptive power he will make it appear that God's special blessing is poured out; there will be manifest what is thought to be great religious interest. Multitudes will exult that God is working marvelously for them, when it comes from another spirit.

"Under a religious guise, Satan will seek to extend his influence over the Christian world" (GC 464).

Call it the Jesus movement, charismatic renewal, faith healing, or whatever, it will content the people with some exciting, emotional experience. At the same time it prevents them from going to the real Source of joy, happiness, deliverance from sin, and security—Jesus—and a relationship of surrender and obedience to Him and to His Word.

Authentic Way of Receiving the Holy Spirit

Is the baptism of the Holy Spirit something that happens in an atmosphere of excitement and emotionalism?

Does the Spirit of the Lord enter a human life regardless of whether or not he or she has a full conversion demonstrated by the fruits of the Spirit and an obedience to the law of God?

The Bible and the writings of Ellen G. White teach that the fullness of the Spirit, the baptism with this heavenly power, will take place after the same Spirit has convicted the sinful heart and after the individual has fully responded to His voice. The full baptism occurs after the Spirit has become an abiding personality in the life and after the Christian has manifested a sincere desire for the Spirit to use him in the kingdom of heaven on earth.

The Christian receives the Spirit not on the basis of feeling and emotion but through secret communion, obedience, and surrender. On the other hand, religious feeling and a supernatural manifestation never guarantee divine origin or approval by God.

Moreover, the reception of the Holy Spirit, like salvation, is not a one-shot deal, something that happens in a person once and forever in a spectacular way so that he stays for all his life baptized in the Spirit. It does not come in the atmosphere of hypersuggestibility that characterizes neo-Pentecostalism. The Christian has to meet the necessary conditions every day, or his life loses that baptism and fullness. Every day he needs a renewal of the experience of repentance and conversion. And every day he must surrender to God to make the Spirit's power permanent in the life.

In the same way our Lord daily received the endowment of the Spirit, after spending the first hours of the morning with God (COL 139). In the quietness of private prayer, after a contemplation of the wonderful character of Jesus, after requesting and receiving by faith both His imputed righteousness and His imparted character, the child of God acquires by faith the daily baptism of the Holy Spirit.

Chapter 10

The Climactic Conflict
of Armageddon

Some of our writers and evangelists have employed
the battle of Armageddon to refer to the division of the
political world into two different factions, some countries aligning with the ideology of the East and others
with that of the West, as a preparation for the events of
the sixth plague.

The only basis for such an assumption comes from
the two following expressions: (1) "That the way of the
kings of the east might be prepared" (Revelation 16:12).
(2) "Go forth unto the kings of the earth and of the whole
world, to gather them to the battle of that great day of
God Almighty. . . . And he gathered them together into a
place called in the Hebrew tongue Armageddon" (verses
14-16).

Such an interpretation, although it captures the public's attention, is not a sound exegesis. Fortunately, the
view never had a complete acceptance among us, and
deeper and more scholarly study of prophecy done by
some of our theologians has shown that it did not have
any Biblical or logical basis. No place in the Bible speaks
of "the kings of the east" fighting with "the kings of the
west." Actually the latter expression does not appear at
all in the context of Armageddon.

Moreover, the idea that there would be a great single
battle or a literal and political war fought in a specific

place called Armageddon and the localization of that place as the Valley of Megiddo in Palestine rests only on a phonetical resemblance between the words *Megiddo* and *Armageddon*. But it is an extremely weak bit of support. In the light of a total study of the prophecy of Revelation 16 with other passages of the Bible and with relevant statements of the writings of Ellen G. White, it becomes completely inadequate. Since the elements mentioned in it are just symbolic, it is logical to assume that the word *Armageddon*, which appears in no other place of the Bible, is not a definite geographical location but a symbolic word.

So, doing away with whatever prejudices we may have had, we will see that every detail of the sixth and the seventh plagues will fall into place when we carefully examine the subject.

We should first point out the fact that the theme of Armegeddon does have vital importance. It arises from Christ's admonition: "Behold, I come as a thief. Blessed is he that watcheth, and keepeth his garments, lest he walk naked, and they see his shame" (Revelation 16:15).

The Time and the Setting of Armegeddon

These words of Jesus, the real author of the Book of Revelation, assume a vital dimension because they remind us that the sixth plague and Armageddon happen during the last hour of the time of trouble. The powerful intervention of God, through Jesus, who will come to destroy His enemies and liberate His people, crowns the event.

Thus we should not and cannot wait to see the prediction's fulfillment in order to determine that we are in the last moments of human history. When the events here prophesied begin to happen, we will be just hours away from the Second Coming. It would be extremely late to make any preparation. When we see the different

powers involved in Armageddon preparing themselves
to make their final thrust against God's people—what we
see dramatically taking place before our eyes right
now—we can know that the end of probationary time
nears and that we are rapidly approaching the pouring
out of the seven last plagues.

The Drying up of the Euphrates, and the Kings of the East

The first verse of the presentation of the sixth plague
is the most controversial one. No unanimous interpretation of it yet exists. But the uncertainty regarding this
part of the prophecy does not make ambiguous any
fundamental aspect of it. All the vital elements are clear,
both from a study of the Bible and of Mrs. White.

Since it is an unfulfilled prophecy, we should be
extremely careful lest we make any dogmatic pro-
nouncement about verse 12, which contains the uncer-
tain aspect. Nevertheless, even verse 12 should not be
hard to understand when we grasp the real meaning of
all the prophecy's components. It declares, "And the
sixth angel poured out his vial upon the great river
Euphrates; and the water thereof was dried up, that the
way of the kings of the east might be prepared."

What does the drying up of the Euphrates mean?
Who are the "kings of the east"?

We would like to select a possible interpretation that
to us seems logical. Evidently the apostle is using symbols. The Euphrates was the river on whose shore the
great city of Babylon stood. From it the city took the
water needed for its survival.

The Bible employs Babylon as a symbol of religious
confusion and spiritual apostasy, and the Book of Revelation elsewhere uses the name to represent Rome, the
headquarters of spiritual confusion and apostasy (Revelation 14:8; 17:5). Water represents peoples and mul-

titudes, nations and tongues (Revelation 17:15). So, one could consider the drying up of the waters of the river a symbol of a change of mind in the multitudes that up to the last moment supported Rome, the spiritual Babylon, as prophesied in Revelation 17:16, 17. And this is what will cause the destruction of the great spiritual Babylon, once it no longer has the allegiance of the people that formerly had worshiped it (Revelation 13:4).

The collapse of support for Babylon would prepare the way of the kings of the east. It is logical to assume that the kings of the east are Christ, the victorious King of kings, and all the armies of heaven that along with Him will fight against the enemies of God and destroy them completely.

What Armageddon Really Is

Seen in this perspective, Armageddon is not a single political war or battle but the final confrontation between Christ and Satan. It will be mainly an ideological or spiritual fight, though it may involve nations and the use of armies to persecute the church of God.

Verses 13 and 14 introduce some of the parties allied with Satan in his final effort to destroy God and His church. They are: (a) unclean spirits, or spirits of demons; (b) the dragon, which in essence, as we have seen elsewhere, is Satan but here manifests himself under spiritism, paganism, and all related practices; (c) the beast, the Papacy, Romanism; (d) the false prophet, that is, the United States once it becomes a persecuting power; (e) the kings or governments of the whole earth (the apostasy and rebellion will be universal, the miracles done by the evil spirits will have deluded all governments [Revelation 16:14]); (f) all the forces act under the direct inspiration and command of Satan and employ the wicked people of the earth.

The other side consists of the following: (a) Christ,

King of kings, the rider on the white horse (Revelation 19:11-16); (b) the holy angels, the armies of heaven; (c) the loyal people of God, the object of the devil's wrath.

The war's immediate object, particularly of its last episode, is to destroy the stubborn minority that resisted the imposition of the mark of the beast, kept their relationship with Jesus fresh and alive, pressed on in the power of the Holy Spirit to spread the knowledge of the gospel to every human being, and remained free from sin through God's strength.

Armageddon will be Satan's fiercest attack, but the battle will end in a complete and eternal victory over him.

It will totally vindicate God's law and completely reestablish His justice in the sight of all the universe.

The Outcome of Armageddon

Revelation 19 presents the outcome of Armageddon: "An angel standing in the sun . . . cried with a loud voice, saying to all the fowls that fly in the midst of heaven, Come and gather yourselves together unto the supper of the great God; that ye may eat the flesh of kings, and the flesh of captains, and the flesh of mighty men, and the flesh of horses, and of them that sit on them" (verses 17, 18).

In the next scene, after watching all the birds consume the great men, the prophet beheld the beast taken captive, along with the false prophet, and he saw the two powers cast alive into a lake of fire with brimstone and the remnant of the enemy armies slain by the sword of Him that sat upon the horse.

The only character missing here is the dragon, Satan. Although by now he also is completely and forever conquered, he is not yet destroyed. This lake of fire is not the same as the one that burns at the end of the millennium. Satan still lives—chained, impotent, in a wasted and destroyed world—to contemplate during the thousand years the ominous results of his revolution. Then the lake of fire that will destroy the last traces of sin and rebellion.

Despair of the Wicked

In the vision of the sixth seal in Revelation 6 John saw that "heaven departed as a scroll when it is rolled together; and every mountain and island were moved out of their places" (verse 14). The tremendous upheavals of nature, indicating the presence of God to rescue His people, terrify the wicked.

"And the kings of the earth, and the great men, and the rich men, and the chief captains, and the mighty men, and every bondman, and every free man, hid themselves in the dens and in the rocks of the mountains; and said to the mountains and rocks, Fall on us, and hide us from the face of him that sitteth on the throne, and from the wrath of the Lamb: for the great day of his wrath is come; and who shall be able to stand?" (verses 15-17).

The description coincides with what the Old Testament prophets wrote about the awesome events immediately preceding the Second Coming (Isaiah 26:21; Zechariah 14:12). They referred to the sense of desperation it will bring to those not prepared, especially the social leaders who forced the mark of the beast on the people, and the religious leaders in whom the deceived multitudes trusted. Regarding them, Mrs. White wrote that as the people turn against them, holding them responsible for their condition, "their suffering was tenfold greater than that of their people" (EW 282).

The Triumphant Faithful

Thank God that among the millions of people who

have aligned themselves with Satan and his hosts, there exists a triumphant group of loyal men and women who in spite of persecution and threat of death, amid general apostasy, remained loyal to their Master and God.

The 144,000 have the name of their Father written on their foreheads. Not defiled with false doctrines, they follow the Lamb wherever He goes. They stand without fault before the throne of God (Revelation 14:4, 5).

All sing of victory and happiness. They have demonstrated before the universe that it was possible to remain without sin during the time of trouble. And their lives prove that Adam and Eve could have perfectly obeyed God's law, which in turn shows Satan's accusation against God that the law was unjust and impossible for man to fulfill was a falsehood.

Because they had human minds and bodies that suffered the effect of six thousand years of sin and degradation, they had had a more difficult time achieving the goal of perfect obedience. But by faith and a total dependence on God's power they kept their covenant with Christ, and now they go to receive their eternal reward.

Now Is the Time

Theoretical knowledge of the facts of the struggle between good and evil and a mental assurance that the King of kings will triumph, and with Him all His people, will not do us much good if we do not manage to be among them. Consequently, before John ends his presentation of the sixth plague, he inserts Jesus' charge: "Behold, I come as a thief. Blessed is he that watcheth, and keepeth his garments, lest he walk naked, and they see his shame" (Revelation 16:15).

Now is the time in which we can give the needed attention to our spiritual condition. In a short while it will be forever late. When the sun of mercy sets and the clouds of the time of trouble gather to spread darkness over the earth, Jesus will no longer be available to give us the only garment that will make us eligible to participate in the wedding feast. The Lord of the house now examines each guest to see if he has that robe.

The robe is not only the imputed righteousness of Christ, received through repentance and forgiveness, but it is also a new heart, a new life of victory and obedience, a rebirth in Christ, which gives us His imparted character. A rebirth implies first a denial of self (Matthew 16:24), the death of the old man (Romans 6:6; Galatians 2:20). Only Christ can liberate us from that old man, and He does it after we make a total surrender (Romans 6:13) and a complete submission (James 4:7). Then He can take over in our lives, making us victorious day by day.

Chapter 11

Liberation of the Church

After six thousand years of struggle we are ready now to behold Heaven's mighty intervention to liberate God's loyal people. The Sun of righteousness is about to rise. The King of the universe is about to manifest Himself in the most dramatic and unusual way, so that all, both the just and the unjust, will proclaim His goodness and justice.

The seventh plague, which we will deal with in this chapter, is the final victory, the glorious crowning of the conflict of Armageddon, which, as we saw, is the last and fiercest attack of the allied persecuting powers against God's children.

The prophetic clock of heaven announces an appointed hour for every great event. When the "fulness of the time" had arrived, God sent His Son to the world for His great mission of salvation (Galatians 4:4). When the right moment came in the timetable of God, our Heavenly High Priest began the second phase of His intercessory work, inaugurating the investigative judgment in the courts above (Daniel 8:14). And when the hour of liberation shall come, a great commotion of the elements of heaven and earth will take place in a fantastic display of divine glory. The forces of evil, ready to destroy the men and women marked by the seal of the living God, will stand paralyzed by a unique demonstration of the power of the Almighty.

One important difference, though, exists between the previous events and this latter one. A time prophecy established the beginning of the investigative judgment. But Scripture reveals no definite prophetic *period* separating us from the *end* of the investigative judgment and the coming of the Lord. We have a definite *task* to accomplish: the perfecting of our characters and the preaching of the gospel to the whole world. But we cannot do either merely through human effort. Both need the powerful working of the Holy Spirit. However, the power of God can work those miracles only upon the fulfillment of the necessary conditions on our part. He needs our complete surrender, our active interest, and our total commitment and collaboration.

"Had Adventists, after the great disappointment in 1844, held fast their faith, and followed on unitedly in the opening providence of God, receiving the message of the third angel and in the power of the Holy Spirit proclaiming it to the world, they would have seen the salvation of God, the Lord would have wrought mightily with their efforts, the work would have been completed, and Christ would have come ere this to receive His people to their reward. . . . It was not the will of God that the coming of Christ should be thus delayed" (1SM 68).

"Christ is waiting with longing desire for the manifestation of Himself in His church. When the character of Christ shall be perfectly reproduced in His people, then He will come to claim them as His own" (COL 69).

In other words, we have the privilege of shortening the waiting time, the history of misery and pain in our world. "By giving the gospel to the world it is in our power to hasten our Lord's return. We are not only to look for but to hasten the coming of the day of God. 2 Peter 2:12, margin. Had the church of Christ done her appointed work as the Lord ordained, the whole world would before this have been warned, and the Lord Jesus

would have come to our earth in power and great glory"
(DA 633, 634).

"Long has God waited for the spirit of service to take
possession of the whole church, so that everyone shall be
working for Him according to his ability. When the
members of the church of God do their appointed work
in the needy fields at home and abroad, in fulfillment of
the gospel commission, the whole world will soon be
warned and the Lord Jesus will return to this earth with
power and great glory" (AA 111).

God has mercifully delayed the liberation hour, waiting for more people to let Him prepare them for His
return. But the delay will come to an end. The church will
complete its revival and reformation, and the unpre-
pared will have finally been sifted out. God will have
finished the gospel mission, and after the short time of
trouble He will speak from heaven through the events of
the seventh plague. The final victory will be an eternal
reality, freeing the happy redeemed ones forever from all
pain and suffering.

The Seventh Plague

Revelation 16:17-21 portrays before our eyes a fantastic display of natural and unnatural phenomena that will
announce the imminent coming of the Lord. The voice of
God speaks audibly from heaven in majestic tones: "It is
done." Finished is salvation and the persecution and
hardships of the saints. In the clock of heaven the hour of
total freedom has struck, and they are about to sing the
song of victory.

Voices and thunders and lightnings accompany a
terrible earthquake, "such as was not since men were
upon the earth." Our minds cannot imagine the scene of
terror and confusion that will instantly halt the wicked in
their attempt to slay the saints.

The great spiritual Babylon was up to now a united

front of apostasy and enmity. But now "the great city was divided into three parts." Every ally pulled apart, and they began fighting against each other in a total disarray. Thus "great Babylon came in remembrance before God, to give unto her the cup of the wine of the fierceness of his wrath." Now all the unseen armies of heaven fight against the wicked powers of demons and men, and the latter begin to drink the wine of God's fierce wrath.

The power of the Almighty stirs up all the elements of nature to produce gigantic cataclysms, and "every island fled away, and the mountains were not found." The surface of the earth radically changes in a short moment. Meanwhile there falls the greatest "hail out of heaven, every stone about the weight of a talent [almost 66 pounds]: and men blasphemed God because of the plague of the hail; for the plague thereof was exceeding great."

The Sun Shines at Midnight

Ellen G. White, guided by the inspiration of the Holy Spirit, has added more details to the events of the seventh plague.

Many of the saints await death in dungeons and prison cells all over the world. The wicked have surrounded the rest of the redeemed in deserts, mountains, and caves. But the situation changes instantly. The voice of God reverberates from heaven, and nature responds. "The foundations of the earth shake; buildings totter and fall with a terrible crash. The sea boils like a pot, and the whole earth is in terrible commotion. The captivity of the righteous is turned, and with sweet and solemn whisperings they say to one another: 'We are delivered. It is the voice of God' " (1T 354).

Part of these events happen at midnight, when the wicked prepare to annihilate the redeemed at one blow:

"It was at midnight that God chose to deliver His people. As the wicked were mocking around them, suddenly the sun appeared, shining in his strength, and the moon stood still. The wicked looked upon the scene with amazement, while the saints beheld with solemn joy the tokens of their deliverance" (EW 285).

The Lord's ways are wonderful. He joyfully delivers when we see no human possibilities. The moments of apparent desperation for man offer Him the opportunity to intervene. When the powerful armies of Egypt, with all their might, poised to destroy the Hebrews, when escape seemed hopeless, God gave them a complete and joyous victory.

And now, "without hand," the wicked shall perish, destroyed by the elements of nature.

Let us remember and relate more often the wonderful chapters of our experience when deliverance came to us personally in dangerous situations, when we were not able to foresee any human solution. But the merciful intervention of God and the ministry of the holy angels rescued us. There is no problem that God does not have a solution for. No temptation or trial can be stronger than the help God will give us, if we only trust and depend on Him within a relationship of surrender and obedience.

The Great Reward

To the people of God in the Laodicean period who have shaken out their indifference and lukewarmness, Christ promises, "To him that overcometh will I grant to sit with me in my throne, even as I also overcame, and am set down with my Father in his throne" (Revelation 3:21). The same promise appears under another symbol in chapter 2:10: "Be thou faithful unto death, and I will give thee a crown of life."

Signs and wonders follow in an uninterrupted succession. The sky looks like a scroll being rolled together, mountains disappear and islands submerge, history's biggest earthquake shakes down huge and proud cities. But the children of God rest secure in the hiding place He provides for them. Isaiah wrote: "Come, my people, enter thou into thy chambers, and shut thy doors about thee: hide thyself as it were for a little moment, until the indignation be overpast. For, behold, the Lord cometh out of his place to punish the inhabitants of the earth for their iniquity" (Isaiah 26:20, 21).

"It Is Done!"

Declared at the beginning of the seventh plague, the announcement "It is done" (1) determines the end of the time of Jacob's trouble, (2) marks the hour of liberation for the redeemed, (3) points to the moment when the real character of the mystery of iniquity has been completely clarified and Satan and his allies totally unmasked. The religious and political forces warring against God's people appear as unveiled representatives of falsehood and satanic delusion. God has allowed them to operate until then to reveal with absolute clarity before the whole universe their real intentions and their origin, and now He delivers His children.

When Jesus was about to die on the cross, thus sealing the plan of redemption and assuring its successful outcome, He exclaimed, "It is finished" (John 19:30). And after declaring that He would re-create the earth as the eternal abode of the redeemed, Christ goes on to say, "It is done" (Revelation 21:6). The Lord will have completed the implementation of His eternal plan of having a happy earth and a perfect universe without any pain or sin. The history of mankind has effectively vaccinated all created beings against the terrible disease. All will have seen clearly the wisdom, the love, and the justice of God, and will serve Him through love forever.

As a result of that divine declaration—"It is done"—

Jesus consummates His plan: "I will that they also, whom thou hast given me, be with me where I am" (John 17:24). The children of God enter the wedding feast. "They come! they come! holy, harmless, and undefiled," Mrs. White writes. "They have kept the word of My patience; they shall walk among the angels" (GC 636). And as they prepare to journey to heaven they shout with a cry of victory.

Cataclysmic Events

The tremendous commotion of nature, manifested in earthquake, hurricane, and hailstone, reveals God's wrath toward the plans of hardened sinners. They have refused His leading, and consequently Satan has used them as his instruments.

As the proud cities of the world crumble, "prison walls are rent asunder, and God's people, who have been held in bondage for their faith, are set free" (GC 637).

Another Sign of the Appearance of the Prince of Life

The psalmist wrote a beautiful description of the confidence the redeemed will have during the world's hour of darkness and turmoil: "God is our refuge and strength, a very present help in trouble. Therefore will not we fear, though the earth be removed, and though the mountains be carried into the midst of the sea; though the waters thereof roar and be troubled, though the mountains shake with the swelling thereof" (Psalm 46:1-3).

Ellen White saw that from the cloudy sky a star suddenly shines. The faces of the loyal minority, up to now pale and anxious in spite of their confidence, now brighten with a feeling of faith and love.

God's voice again resounds in impressive tones, announcing the day and the hour of the actual coming of

Jesus, and an expression of glory covers the faces of the redeemed. Soon there appears the cloud that surrounds the coming Saviour.

Only the grace of God prepared them for salvation, and only through Christ and His righteousness will they be ready to inherit heaven. They have received through faith the white raiment for their forgiveness and justification, and for their victory over sin and defects of character. And now, when they ask with trembling voices, "Who shall be able to stand?" Jesus proclaims, "My grace is sufficient for you."

The final liberation is done. The sorrows and pains are in the past. Now heaven and life eternal with their Master seem too great a reward for such a small sacrifice. They join the choir of celestial hosts in singing to the honor and glory of God: "Blessing, and glory, and wisdom, and thanksgiving, and honour, and power, and might, be unto our God for ever and ever. Amen" (Revelation 9:12).

Chapter 12

The Second Coming and the 144,000

Man's history on earth has two outstanding focal points: the first advent of Christ, which divided history in two and was the summit of the plan of redemption; and His second coming, which culminates God's restorative process.

The first event came at history's darkest hour. The life and death of Christ was the brightest light of heaven shining in humanity's blackest night.

The Second Coming will take place when the powers of evil seem about to destroy God's plans and to strike a deadly blow against the ransomed. At that precise hour God's glory will be seen in heaven, and He will carry out His eternal purpose in the most dramatic demonstration of His power.

Main Events Leading to the Second Coming

The happenings of the sixth plague have stopped the wicked from slaying the righteous, and while its former supporters attack the fallen Babylon and fight against each other, there appears in the sky a small cloud made up of all the holy angels, with Jesus in its center riding in glory.

Partial resurrection. Daniel saw that "many of them that sleep in the dust of the earth shall awake, some to everlasting life, and some to shame and everlasting contempt" (Daniel 12:2). And John wrote, "He cometh with clouds; and every eye shall see him, and they also which pierced him" (Revelation 1:7). It is a special limited resurrection previous to the general one of all the dead in Christ that will happen a little later.

The graves of some of the dead saints and of some of the most wicked men open in the partial resurrection. Ellen White described it: "Dark, heavy clouds came up and clashed against each other. But there was one clear place of settled glory, whence came the voice of God like many waters, shaking the heavens and the earth. There was a mighty earthquake. The graves were opened, and those who had died in faith under the third angel's message, keeping the Sabbath, came forth from their dusty beds, glorified, to hear the covenant of peace that God was to make with those who had kept His law. . . . Their countenances were lighted up with the glory of God, and they shone with glory as did the face of Moses when he came down from Sinai" (EW 285, 286). Thus some will rise to everlasting life at this time. Those who died during the preaching of the third angel's message will be among them.

But others will rise "to shame and everlasting contempt," including those "also which pierced him." "Those that mocked and derided Christ's dying agonies, and the most violent opposers of His truth and His people, are raised to behold Him in His glory and to see the honor placed upon the loyal and obedient" (GC 637).

A hand in heaven holding the two tables of the law. In the sky, while the commotions of the sixth plague continue, there appears a hand that opens the tables of the law, and humanity sees the commandments of God as clearly as if they were traced with a pen of fire (GC 639).

The actual appearance of the King of kings. The ransomed immediately interpret the small cloud, about half the size of a man's hand, as the cloud of innumerable angels that surround Christ's throne. Its size keeps increasing as it brightens.

Soon it becomes a great bright cloud. Christ rides on it, sitting on a white throne, and the rainbow of the covenant shines on top of it. A huge cluster of angels— actually all the angels of heaven—accompany their Master and King.

While He makes His majestic descent upon the cloud, the atmosphere rolls back like a scroll, and the earth trembles. The words of Psalm 50:3, 4 are fulfilled: "Our God shall come, and shall not keep silence: a fire shall devour before him, and it shall be very tempestuous round about him. He shall call to the heavens from above, and to the earth, that he may judge his people."

Meanwhile, the wicked plead for the mountains to bury them and hide them from Christ's face.

The general resurrection of the righteous. At that moment all the dead in Christ, of all ages from Adam on, rise from the grave immortal and incorruptible (1 Thessalonians 4:17). At the same time God completely transforms the living redeemed (1 Corinthians 15:51, 52), and both groups together soar up into the clouds to meet their Lord (1 Thessalonians 4:17).

But the brightness of Christ's coming destroys the wicked (2 Thessalonians 2:8).

The song of victory and praise. While the Saviour and His angels lead the redeemed toward heaven they sing a song of praise and victory, whose refrain is: "Unto him that loved us, and washed us from our sins in his own blood, and hath made us kings and priests unto God and his Father; to him be glory and dominion for ever and ever" (Revelation 1:5, 6).

The One Hundred Forty-four Thousand

Among the happy multitude of men, women, and children of all ages that will greet the glorious coming of

Christ there exists a special group designated as the 144,000. Revelation 7 and 14 presents them.

We will try to explain four aspects about them: (1) when they appear and act, (2) who they are, (3) their characteristics and marks of identification, (4) their special activities.

When they appear in the scene. They entered Mrs. White's vision, recorded in *Early Writings,* a little before the dark cloud that afterward became the bright host of angels (EW 15). She also mentions them before the general resurrection of the saints. After viewing the privileged group she heard the trumpet of Jesus, and the graves opened for the dead in Christ to arise (EW 16). The 144,000 recognized some friends that had died before the time of trouble (EW 16).

Mrs. White makes an interesting statement that they heard the voice of God announcing the Saviour's coming: "Soon we heard the voice of God like many waters, which gave us the day and hour of Jesus' coming. The living saints, 144,000 in number, knew and understood the voice, while the wicked thought it was thunder and an earthquake" (EW 15).

Who and how many they are. First of all, we know that all the living redeemed who pass through the time of trouble will be among them. All of them will be sealed children of God and perfectly united in their faith (EW 15).

When we consider the glories of the future and the great privilege we will have of beholding with our own eyes the wonderful face of Jesus and hearing with our own ears His melodious and majestic voice, all earthly attractions fade, and we say with Paul, "I count all things but loss for the excellency of the knowledge of Christ Jesus my Lord: for whom I have suffered the loss of all things, and do count them but dung, that I may win Christ" (Philippians 3:8). Position, honor, money, pleasure, rank and hierarchy, supremacy: such things are but dung compared with the blessing of being with Jesus.

But in order to be a part of that group we must have perfect union with each other. We must not have hard feelings or strife for ascendancy. Such a meek and humble spirit we can acquire only at the feet of Jesus, who said, "Come unto me. . . . Take my yoke upon you, and learn of me; for I am meek and lowly in heart" (Matthew 11:28, 29).

Because it is one of the hardest traits to incorporate into our character, we can hope to get it only by divesting ourselves of self. Every day through private prayer we must request God's strength. Then we would be taking to heart Paul's admonition: "Let this mind [spirit] be in you, which was also in Christ Jesus" (Philippians 2:5).

Aside from the living redeemed that go through the trouble of Jacob's time, there is a possibility that some of the dead in Christ may be among the 144,000. We have two statements in mind that may suggest this.

The first one appears in *Early Writings*, page 40. An angel told Mrs. White in a vision, "You must go back, and if you are faithful, *you, with the 144,000*, shall have the privilege of visiting all the worlds and viewing the handiwork of God." Whether the language of the angel means that Mrs. White will be part of the group, or whether, along with the group, she will have some of the same privileges, we do not know.

The second occurs in *Selected Messages*, Book Two, page 263. Ellen White assures a bereaved husband, "I saw that she [the deceased wife] was sealed and would come up at the voice of God and stand upon the earth, and *would be with the 144,000*." Here again we do not know whether the semantics mean that the woman would belong to the 144,000 or whether she will be along with them and enjoy some of their benefits.

Other than that, neither the Bible nor Ellen White reveals much to us.

About the exact number we have no unanimity either. Some consider the figure as a literal one, probably designating the heads of families without taking into consideration the women and the children, as in the case of the five thousand fed by Christ.

Others—including the author of this book—prefer to consider it a symbolic number. The vision of Revelation 7 and 14 is evidently symbolic. The women, the virgins, the Lamb, the firstfruits, all are symbols. So it would be consistent if we consider the figure also a symbol.

God is not ruled by mathematics, and He cannot limit Himself and His power to a restricted and exact figure. What if there should be one or two more than 144,000 prepared for translation? Would He then leave them without eternal life because the number has been reached?

The tribes of Israel also are symbolic. It is not the physical or literal Israel that the Book of Revelation speaks about, but spiritual Israel, today scattered over the whole earth and including members of every race. Twelve thousand from every tribe means simply an immense number from every nation and tongue and race, belonging to all backgrounds. The gospel of Christ is the power of God to convert the heart of anybody, regardless of nationality or heredity.

Whatever our views on the nature of the 144,000, we should always remember the following advice Mrs. White wrote: "When men pick up this theory and that theory [in regard to the 144,000], when they are curious to know something it is not necessary for them to know, God is not leading them. It is not His plan that His people shall present something which they have to suppose, which is not taught in the Word. It is not His will that they shall get into controversy over questions which will not help them spiritually, such as, Who is to compose the hundred and forty-four thousand? This those who are the elect of God will in a short time know without question" (1SM 174).

The main purpose of the passages presenting the number is not to reveal a precise figure but to signify a worldwide distribution.

Marks of identification of the 144,000. The important aspect of our study is to know what characteristics they will have so that we can ask God to give them to us.

1. They are "redeemed from the earth" (Revelation 14:3). Responding to the great price paid for them, they have separated from the world as children of God in a special hour of history.

2. They are sealed (Revelation 7:4). In other words, they have obtained victory over sin and a stained character so that the angels could put on them the seal of the living God. That seal represents a perfect law written in the heart, the perfect character of God imparted to them by faith. They have been so established in a sound and permanent experience with God that they can pass through the time of trouble without a Mediator, through having learned to depend on Christ and His power.

3. The name of the Father is "written on their foreheads" (Revelation 14:1, RSV). "On their foreheads was written, God, New Jerusalem, and a glorious star containing Jesus' new name" (EW 15). The name of the Father is the general name, the last name, the family name, given to them because they have been adopted as children of God. But along with it they receive a specific "new name, . . . which no man knoweth saving he that receiveth it" (Revelation 2:17). No one else knows his new name because it arises from a particular experience that has developed definite traits the individual needed in order to have a character similar to Christ's.

4. "Not defiled with women; . . . they are virgins" (Revelation 14:4). They avoided false doctrines, spurious churches, and forbidden activities, which Scripture equates with idolatry.

5. "In their mouth was found no guile." They are

truthful in every respect, because "the Lord hates . . . a lying tongue" (Proverbs 6:16, 17) and because "He is . . . a God of truth" (Deuteronomy 32:4), being Himself the personification of truth in the person of His Son (John 14:6).

6. "They are without fault" (Revelation 14:5). Normally we speak about relative perfection, about a process of growth and spiritual maturation. But here the passage refers to a sinless state, to a blameless life. No longer is it wishful thinking, but a consummated fact. John saw that the 144,000 were without fault. And if it is a fact beheld by the apostle, it indicates that God can provide us with the means to achieve it.

No human power or personal effort is sufficient for it. But when we put our lives unconditionally into God's hands, He will produce new perfect ones, which requires nothing less than a great miracle of the Holy Spirit.

The generation living at the second coming of Jesus will have reached such an experience. The Holy Spirit will keep them sinless. And they demonstrate before the entire universe that the ideal God had established at the beginning—a perfect obedience to a perfect and holy law—is a total possibility.

7. The suffering they will go through during the time of trouble will even take their characters to a higher state of perfection. "These are they which came out of great tribulation" (Revelation 7:14). "They have passed through the time of trouble such as never was since there was a nation; they have endured the anguish of the time of Jacob's trouble. . . . They have seen the earth wasted with famine and pestilence, the sun having power to scorch men with great heat, and they themselves have endured suffering, hunger, and thirst" (GC 649).

Activities of the 144,000. First of all, they sing a new song, a song that nobody except them can learn because it represents their unique experience. It is a song of victory, of joy, of deliverance (Revelation 14:2, 3).

They follow the Lamb wherever He goes (Revelation 14:4). Only they will enter the temple of Zion. "As we were about to enter the holy temple, Jesus raised His lovely voice and said, 'Only the 144,000 enter this place,' and we shouted, 'Alleluia' " (EW 19).

Inside they found stone tablets engraved in gold with the names of the 144,000. Immediately Jesus said, "Come, My people, you have come out of great tribulation, and done My will; suffered for Me; come in to supper, for I will gird Myself, and serve you." She saw "a table of pure silver . . . many miles in length," with all kinds of beautiful and delicious fruits. In spite of its length her eyes could perceive everything on it (EW 19).

And finally, Mrs. White mentioned the group would visit other planets: "The Lord has given me a view of other worlds. Wings were given me, and an angel attended me from the city to a place that was bright and glorious" (EW 39). And she relates the interesting conversation she had with one of its inhabitants.

To Assure Our Participation in That Glorious Meeting

Obviously we can obtain the marks of identification possessed by the 144,000 only through a full surrender to God. "Submit yourselves therefore to God. Resist the devil, and he will flee from you" (James 4:7). Without Christ we can do nothing (John 15:5). But with Him everything is possible (Philippians 4:13).

Chapter 13

Christ, Our Victory

After reviewing in the former chapters the awesome events that will soon shake the world and perplex the church of God, it is natural and proper to raise a question similar to the one asked by the psalmist: "Who shall ascend into the hill of the Lord? or who shall stand in his holy place?" (Psalm 24:3).

How do we prepare ourselves?

The tendency of many of us who compose Laodicea is to unwittingly consider ourselves endowed with all the qualities needed for translation, just because we as a church have special insights and we as individuals are acquainted with them and handle them fairly well. Without doubt we have ample reasons to thank God for the great privilege of possessing spiritual truth. The message to Laodicea does not condemn us for heresy or falsehood.

But an intellectual understanding, the ability to explain Biblical doctrines, will not save anybody. We must always remember that fact. Only then may we be able to see ourselves as we are, spiritually poor and in need of everything. It is the only attitude that would assure us access to God's power. When in the day of judgment some will tell God, "Lord, Lord, have we not prophesied in thy name? and in thy name have cast out devils? and in thy name done many wonderful works?" Jesus will answer, "I never knew you: depart from me, ye that work iniquity" (Matthew 7:22, 23). We find the reason for His strange reply in the previous verse: "Not every one that saith unto me, Lord, Lord, shall enter into the kingdom of heaven; but he that doeth the will of my Father which is in heaven."

Life, and not profession, is the measure. Deeds, and not words, are the test. Experience, and not mere knowledge, is the condition.

But again the same question remains: How do we reach a really converted life, a genuine new experience, the character of Christ? There is just one answer, only one way. The secret is Christ—Christ living and working in us.

An Experiential Knowledge

There are two different ways of knowing somebody. One way is to read a lot about him, to hear and learn about him through other people. The other way involves dealing directly with him, spending time talking with him, and seeing how he reacts to life's different problems.

A man once read a lot about a famous personality. So when in his travels he happened to reach the city where the individual lived, he asked for an appointment, and went to the man's home to have an interview with him. At the house a young man offered the visitor a seat in the waiting room. The traveler, meanwhile, tried to express his admiration for the celebrity. The boy, though much more simple in his observations, said so many interesting things about the man that it amazed the visitor. Finally he told the lad, who he thought was an employee in the house, "I have read so much about So-and-So, but I am surprised how much more you know about him!"

"Well, sir, you know, I am his son," the boy answered simply.

We need the same kind of direct firsthand knowledge about God our Father and about Jesus our Saviour and older Brother. "Thus saith the Lord," writes Jeremiah, "let not the wise man glory in his wisdom, neither let the mighty man glory in his might, let not the rich man glory in his riches: but let him that glorieth glory in this, that he understandeth and knoweth me" (Jeremiah 9:23, 24). If there is any kind of knowledge really worthwhile in the world, it is the experiential knowledge of God.

Christ expressed the same fundamental principle when He said, "This is life eternal, that they might know thee the only true God, and Jesus Christ, whom thou has sent" (John 17:3).

It is the only kind of knowledge that has the power to convert our life, because it puts us in close contact and in a personal relationship with Christ. It changed John's life until he could say, "That which was from the beginning, which we have heard, which we have seen with our eyes, which we have looked upon, and our hands have handled. . . . [I] declare . . . unto you, that ye also may have fellowship with us: and truly our fellowship is with the Father, and with His Son Jesus Christ" (1 John 1:1-3). That direct and daily fellowship with Jesus, that vital relationship with the Master, had transformed a man of selfish and impetuous disposition into the most intimate disciple of the Master, the apostle of love.

When we can speak about the mercy, the forgiveness, and especially the power, of Christ as something we have seen with our own eyes, have heard with our own ears, have felt and handled with our own hands, have seen in action in our own life, we have reached the essence of Christianity. Only then will we speak with authority, because our life, our words, our thoughts, and our feelings are a living testimony of the efficacy of the gospel.

Then our words will echo those of Mrs. White: "I needed help, and I found it in Jesus. Every want was supplied, the hunger of my soul was satisfied; the Bible is to me the revelation of Christ. I believe in Jesus because He is to me a divine Saviour. I believe the Bible because I have found it to be the voice of God to my soul" (MH 461).

A Personal Relationship

There can be no substitute for a personal relationship with God and with Jesus. Paul expressed the wonderful results of that kind of contact with the divine when he said, "If any man be in Christ, he is a new creature: old things are passed away; behold, all things are become new" (2 Corinthians 5:17). The union of our soul with the person of Christ, the total identification of our being with His, produces a real Christian.

The same apostle reduced the secret of the mystery of godliness to three significant words: "Christ in you" (Colossians 1:27). After Christ called him on the road to Damascus, after he acknowledged the voice of the Saviour and responded to it, he spent three years in the desert of Arabia doing nothing else than studying the Word, speaking with Him, until he knew what "Christ in you" meant.

In John 15:4, 5 the Master taught His disciples how vitally important it was for them to have a daily relationship with Him. The life of the branch derives absolutely from the vine. It must be connected to it to receive nourishment, thus producing growth, beautiful flowers, and rich fruit. The moment that anything cuts the branch from the stock, death begins. In a few hours it withers away, and after a few days it is completely dead.

Christ's Rulership of Our Life

In the spiritual kingdom there can be no possibility of life without death first. The "old man" must die in order for the new man to be born. Self must disappear in order for Christ to occupy the heart. There cannot be two kings in the life; it is either self or Christ. And since Christ does not force His entrance into the life, we must let Him in.

One day two discouraged disciples traveled the road to Emmaus when a seeming stranger joined them. He explained the Scriptures, particularly the Messianic prophecies, to them. Finally the disciples arrived home. They invited the unknown companion to come into their house to spend the night with them. At first He acted as though He wanted to go on farther. But they persisted in their invitation. "They constrained him, saying, Abide with us; for it is toward evening, and the day is far spent. And he went in to tarry with them" (Luke 24:28, 29).

Because they persuaded Christ to come into their home, they had a wonderful experience. Being in close contact with Him, they soon discovered that He was Jesus. So when He disappeared, nobody could detain them. They defied darkness, hunger, and weariness, and hurried back to convey the news to their fellow disciples.

Jesus never forces Himself into our lives. If we are not sincerely interested in His companionship, if we do not feel our need of Him and urge Him to enter, He leaves. And what a terrible loss! Nevertheless, Jesus longs to enter into our hearts and into our homes to reside with us.

The only way of knowing the real core of Christian experience, of feeling happiness, courage, rest, and enthusiasm, is by inviting Christ to remain with us so that He may be not only our Saviour but also our Ruler.

"I have been crucified with Christ" (Galatians 2:20, RSV), Paul wrote. There can be no resurrection of a new creature in Christ if first we are not crucified with Him. "It is no longer I who live [self is dead], but Christ who lives in me."

Christian life, salvation, preparation for the coming

of the Lord, requires a constant effort, a conscious perseverance, an active interest, a permanent conflict, against
self. "So long as we are in the world, we shall meet with
adverse influences. There will be provocations to test the
temper; and it is by meeting these in a right spirit that
the Christian graces are developed. If Christ dwells in
us, we shall be patient, kind, and forbearing, cheerful
amid frets and irritations. Day by day and year by year
we shall conquer self, and grow into a noble heroism.
This is our alloted task; but it cannot be accomplished
without help from Jesus, resolute decision, unwavering
purpose, continual watchfulness, and unceasing prayer.
Each one has a personal battle to fight. Not even God can
make our characters noble or our lives useful unless we
become co-workers with Him. Those who decline the
struggle lose the strength and joy of victory" (MH 487).

Christ to Control Our Thoughts

Another aspect of the presence of Christ in our hearts
in order to rule our thoughts and our life appears in the
following statement:

"Christ dwelling in our hearts by faith means the
contemplation of Christ, beholding Christ, ever cherish-
ing the dear Saviour as our very best and honored
Friend, so that we would not in any action grieve and
offend Him. . . . We are abiding in Christ by a living
faith. . . . As the mind dwells upon Christ, the character
is molded after the divine similitude. The thoughts are
pervaded with a sense of His goodness, His love. We
contemplate His character, and thus He is in all our
thoughts. His love encloses us. If we gaze even a moment
upon the sun in its meridian glory, when we turn away
our eyes, the image of the sun will appear in everything
upon which we look. Thus it is when we behold Jesus;
everything we look upon reflects His image, the Sun of
Righteousness. We cannot see anything else, or talk of

anything else. His image is imprinted upon the eye of the soul and affects every portion of our daily life, softening and subduing our whole nature. By beholding, we are conformed to the divine similitude, even the likeness of Christ. . . .

"We cannot, then, center our thoughts upon self; it is no more we that live, but Christ that liveth in us, and He is the hope of glory. Self is dead, but Christ is a living Saviour. Continuing to look unto Jesus, we reflect His image to all around us. We cannot stop to consider our disappointments, or even to talk of them; for a more pleasant picture attracts our sight—the precious love of Jesus" (TM 387-390).

The Role of the Will—Surrender

In the surrender of ourselves to Christ the will has a vital part to play. Actually it is such an important subject that we made extensive research in Scripture and the Ellen White books and found hundreds of paragraphs and quotations dealing with it. But in the short space we have here we will attempt to give the essence of the main ideas. We classified our findings under four subheads:

1. *Definition of man's will.* Among the several meanings that the word has in the dictionary, we use it only in the sense that Mrs. White employed: the deciding power working in man (Ed 289). It is the governing power present in man's nature (MH 176; Ed 289; SC 47). The will is the power of choice that man possesses (ML 318; MH 176).

Will has the idea of freedom of choice, and according to the plan of God it involves a free moral agent. It is one of the most precious attributes put by God in human nature because man was made in the image of his Maker.

2. *Insufficient by itself.* In his present sinful nature, man no longer has the capacity to change his condition from sinful to sinless merely through voluntary choice.

"Man cannot transform himself by the exercise of his will. He possesses no power by which this change can be effected. The leaven—something wholly from without—must be put into the meal before the desired change can be wrought in it. So the grace of God must be received by the sinner before he can be fitted for the kingdom of glory" (COL 96).

3. *Man needs to exercise the will.* God expects man to use his power of choice to renounce sin and accept God for several reasons: (a) God cannot save man against his will. Man needs to open the door of his heart (Revelation 3:20; SD 182). (b) Breaking a person's will is against the principles of heaven (CT 116). (c) Even angels have no right to control or to force man's will (EW 221; MYP 53; 2SG 277, 278). (d) "God does not design that our will should be destroyed, for it is only through its exercise that we can accomplish what He would have us to do" (MB 62). (e) The will is implanted in human nature for a holy purpose (3T 84). It is an important factor in character formation (5T 515).

4. *Subjection of the will to God.* But in order for the human will to perform its holy purpose and develop character, the individual must subject or submit it wholly to God and to Christ (4T 215; AH 213; MB 62). (a) Christ blends man's will to God's will without violence or compulsion (ML 340). (b) Thus God's will becomes man's (5T 515; 1SM 338; 7BC 909). (c) "As the will of man co-operates with the will of God, it becomes omnipotent. Whatever is to be done at His command may be accomplished in His strength. All His biddings are enablings" (COL 333). (d) Christ must have the entire management of man's will (5T 219). (e) God asks man to give Him his will (5T 514, 515). (f) Surrender of our will to God is necessary (2SM 212). (g) By yielding his will to Christ, man allies himself with divine power (MH 176).

The task of submission demands perseverance. "Decided perseverance in a course of righteousness, disciplining the mind by religious exercises to love devotion and heavenly things, will bring the greatest amount of happiness" (2T 507).

Ellen White told one man, "God brought you where your surroundings would be changed and where you could be disciplined by His Holy Spirit, that you might acquire moral power and self-control to make you a conqueror. It will require the strongest effort, the most persevering and unfaltering determination, and the strongest energy to control self" (4T 92).

What a consolation, when we are going through apparently interminable trials and provocations, to know that God permits such conditions that the Holy Spirit may discipline us to give us the victory over self. Instead of complaining and getting discouraged, we should thank God and be ready to learn what the Heavenly Teacher wants us to learn.

The Great Source of Life

God and Christ are the only source of spiritual life, and there is no better way of getting in contact with them than the Written Word. "The words that I have spoken to you are spirit and life" (John 6:63, RSV). Did the disciples not feel it when Jesus conversed with them on the road to Emmaus, and did their hearts not respond, kindled by a new life, when He opened to them the Scriptures? Nothing can make our hearts burn with new life, new enthusiasm, new joy, new hope, and new determination as the study of the Word of God, whether it be in the Bible or portrayed in the writings of Ellen G. White. We are never the same after a quiet, unhurried hour of prayerful meditation, applying to our own life the words of truth and hearing the voice of the Holy Spirit speaking to our hearts.

Among the different weapons mentioned by Paul as part of God's spiritual armor we find: "Praying always with all prayer and supplication in the Spirit, and watching thereunto with all perseverance" (Ephesians 6:18).

After we have been immersed in the thoughts of God, we feel our hearts full of praise and gratitude to our Father for all His love and mercy while the Spirit applies to our own particular needs the written truth. Then we experience a deep longing for godliness, self-control, and spiritual victory. Now we are ready to pray more meaningfully, with more fervor, and from a sense of need. And Christ's promise to those who hunger and thirst for righteousness is that He will satisfy them.